Confessions of a Cross-Bearer

Confessions of a Cross-Bearer

**by
Charles Hodge
&
Eddie Messer**

20th Century Christian Foundation
2809 Granny White Pike
Nashville, Tennessee
37204

Table of Contents

Chapter One

I Have No Greater Joy

"I have no greater joy than to hear that my children walk in truth."
3 John 4

Introduction

JOY!!! If you were asked to name ten outstanding Christian principles, what would they be? Love, humility, courage, faith? Would joy make the list? Is joy the neglected principle? To work is one thing; to work joyously is another. Servanthood is beautiful but only if it is done with joy. To serve grudgingly, to work only from duty destroys ministry. "God loves a joyous worker." How can one cooperate with harsh associates? Only if the lubricant of joy is there! How can one continue when disappointment abounds? Only when joy is there. Joy is the "grease", the "shock absorber" of Christianity. Beware of "Joy Robbers". It is a crime to steal joy from Christians. Don't turn the "Good News" (Gospel) into "Bad News". We will do anything for the Gospel . . . we will preach it, live it, die for it . . . everything but enjoy it! Christianity is joy; sad Christianity is a contradiction. Too many are miserable, doubtful, and uncertain. To them Christianity is like going to a dentist — it is good for you but it is supposed to hurt. Evangelism is not merely sharing our doctrine but equally our joy. Sinners are already miserable! They need the cross — not doom and gloom. They need not only to hear but to see this in our lives. Christians can both save and enjoy the world at the same time. Joy — not grit — is the hallmark of Christian obedience. Joy is the product of grace. You have never seen a "humble liberal" or "happy legalist"! They do not exist; they cannot exist. "Blessed is the people that know the joyful sound" (Psalms 89:15). We are God's people but much of the time one could hardly know it. Joy and Christianity must be synonymous.

Jesus Christ And Joy

When Jesus was born the angels announced joy (Luke 2:8-14). His life was a life of joy. As He prepared to die He said, "These things have I spoken unto you, that my joy might remain in you, and that your joy might be full" (John 15:11). Jesus lived the principle that we are here to glorify God and enjoy Him forever. The joy of Jesus angered the Pharisees. Not only was He good — He enjoyed it! They crucified Him. To serve men for your sake or their sakes will result in bitterness. But to serve for Christ's sake gives joy. Jesus died upon the cross in joy (Heb. 12:1, 2). We sow in tears to reap in joy (Psalms 126:5, 6).

1

Paul And Joy

Paul had much to say/command about joy. The sweetest epistles were written from jails. His command over and over was "rejoice". Philippians is called his sweetest epistle. Paul used one form of joy 14 times in 104 verses! This ratio is over 1 in 10! The fruit of the Spirit is joy (Gal. 5:22). The kingdom of God is joy (Rom. 14:17).

In Romans 12, 1 Corinthians 12, and Ephesians 4, Paul addresses the various functions/works individual Christians have. We correctly teach that each Christian employ (use) his particular gift. But have we also observed these gifts were given to be enjoyed! Joy is with certainty; joy is being where God wants us to be and doing what God wants us to do. Joy is not merely in knowing "who" you are but "whose" you are. The importance of anything you have is enjoying it.

Joy In Pain

What is joy? Joy is not pleasure, fun, superficial happiness. It is not the error that Christians are given a pain-free life. Joy is not a "happy pill". Christians are holy; happiness/joy are by-products. Joy is not what you have but who you are. The glory of Christianity is joy midst pain. James said that we count trials as joy (James 1:2-4); the writer of Hebrews affirmed that discipline with pain resulted in joy (Heb. 12:11). Jesus went into detail in John 16:20-24. He said that sorrow would be turned into joy. The illustration is that of a woman giving birth to a son. Jesus said that no man could take joy away; He also said His joy would be full! This is the depth and reality of joy. The God of hope fills us with joy (Rom. 15:13); we rejoice in the Lord always (Phil. 4:4). Where is our "glow"? Do Christians have something no one else has?

There is joy in challenge. In Oberammergau, Germany, there is a lodge midway up the mountain. Tourists go there by bus. They are invited to walk to the summit. Few do. Most remain safe at the lodge. Those who accepted the challenge returned happy; those who did not returned unhappy. This involves the joy of excellence. Paul said the Macedonian liberality in giving came from joy and not duty (2 Cor. 8:2).

Joy In Others

This is our text and emphasis. Joy is selfless! It concerns others. My joy is in your joy. There cannot be joy in selfishness; this is self-defeating. Those who pursue joy never find it. Paul called the Church at Philippi his joy and crown (Phil. 4:1). He prayed for them in joy (Phil. 1:4); his joy for them was in their faith (Phil. 1:25); their faithfulness fulfilled his joy (Phil. 2:2). Parents' greatest joy is in the goodness of their children; teachers' greatest satisfaction is with their students. This is the real pay in preaching,

2

teaching, and eldering. To see the growth of brethren. Paul said basically the same thing to the Thessalonian. "Ye are our glory and joy" (I Thess. 1:19, 20). Paul's joy was for their sakes (1 Thess. 3:9). Joy, therefore, is a lifestyle — prayers and ministry and concern for others. This is the confession of a disciple.

John says this joy is in their walking in truth. There are several observations to be made: (1) Truth is not merely to be debated — it is to be lived. Excellence in truth is not in debate but conduct. Truth makes a man think like God and act like God. Truth is not assent to a creed but abundant life in Christ (John 10:10). John had just affirmed, "Beloved, I wish above all things that thou mayest prosper and be in health, even as thy soul prospereth" (2 John 2). Apostasy, apathy break a disciple's heart! Zeal in faith produces joy untold! (2) To walk is not to be perfect. This we must grasp. One cannot be faultless; he can be blameless. Walking is a direction, a lifestyle. To be blameless means integrity. John wrote that their joy might be full (1 John 1:4). "Strengthened with all might, according to his glorious power, unto all patience and longsuffering with joyfulness" (Col. 1:11). *JOY!!!* The missing ingredient! The neglected principle. It comes only by the cross; it comes only in discipleship.

Walk In Truth

Our joy is in our "walk". Our joy is not that our children and friends are prospering but that their prosperity is in Christ! Joy comes from knowing that God has chosen us, loved us, and died for us. This means that joy is not something Christians receive at a later date. Joy is now (present) or not at all! Since joy is not dependent upon circumstances there is no excuse for not having it now! Joy is not when "all the ducks are lined up right" . . . when you get the kids raised or retire! Joy comes in walking in truth! Someone has called this, "God's F.A.T. members" . . . Faithful, available, and teachable.

FAITHFUL. This does not mean energetic persistence. Neurotic zeal may not be faith at all. Faithful is simply "full of faith". Faith is in the object not the believing. Believing in believing is absurd. We walk in truth — not merely facts, creed, the right answers to selected questions. Our faith is in truth, reality, concept. God is the "Banker for our life". Faith is not pop psychology, will power. Christians have "Christ-power", "faith-power". Christians live by faith and not by sight (2 Cor. 5:7).

AVAILABLE. The Church is enammered with size, talent, potential. Coach Bear Bryant observed, "No one ever won a ball game on potential". The great issue in life is simply "showing up". Nothing can be done until we show up! The "One-talent Man" was condemned, not because he did not have five, but because the one he had was not available. Joy comes when talents are given God.

3

The people miserable in their religion are the people who are not available. Bloom where you are planted; use what you have. It has yet to be seen what God can do if one gives himself totally to God! The great need is not ability but availability.

TEACHABLE. God can only use men with faith who make themselves available. Paul said he had not arrived (Phil. 3:11–17). Paul kept studying. Many preachers stop studying; some actually never started studying. They got by on youth and future potential. God cannot use "know-it-alls". One who ceases to be a student is disqualified to teach. "Know-it-alls" are miserable. Students of truth find joy. There is no greater joy than in learning, changing,maturing.

Are you faithful? available? teachable?

> I came to Jesus as I was
> Weary and worn and sad.
> I found in Him a resting place.
> And He has made me glad.

Questions

1. Discuss ten outstanding Christian virtues. Notice how basically the same few are given. Is joy on the list? If not, why not? Have we preached grit not joy? Discuss.
2. In our evangelism do we preach Christ or only what we wish sinners to hear? Angels were joyous with Christ but not with creed. Discuss this.
3. From where did Paul write the sweetest epistles? What is the hallmark virtue of Christianity?
4. Can there be joy midst pain? Discuss. Are we asking too much or too little of our children/members?
5. With whom have you shared your joy? Can you rejoice with others in their joy?
6. Is truth mere facts? What is truth? What is the missing ingredient today in many Christians' lives?
7. Who are God's "F.A.T. Members"? Discuss. Are you studying, thinking, maturing?

Chapter Two

I Am Your Servant

" . . . but I am among you as he that serveth."

Luke 22:27

Introduction

SERVANTHOOD!!! A better translation would be, "I am among you as the serving man. The basic nature of God is revealed in Jesus as servanthood. Who were Paul and Barnabus? Servants! (1 Cor. 3:1-9). They started at God's highest rank — servants. Every member a minister (servant). You do not work your way up in Christ — you start at the top — serving. *SERVE - SERVE - SERVE!* The key to understanding Corinthians is 1 Cor. 1:9, "fellowship of Jesus Christ". Focus upon Christ. The power/destiny is Christ. The church is to reproduce Christ. Christians have the mind of Christ (Phil. 2:5-11). The mind of Christ is the mind of a servant.

The Towel

Read John 13. The disciples assemble. Custom said the lowest servant washed feet. None volunteered. Proud minds result in dirty feet. No disciple volunteered to be abased. It is easier to "lord" than serve. It is easier to control than contribute; it is easier to talk rather than listen. The twelve argued over who was greatest. Midst this disgrace Jesus picked up a towel! The last "object lesson" of Jesus was menial service. The disciples did not wish to discuss it; Jesus gives into action.

Only the secured can serve! Jesus knew where He came from, who He was, and where He was going. Insecurity cannot serve. The only thing in life is service. It is one thing to choose to serve; it is another to be a servant. Choosers are still in control. A servant gives up his right to be in charge. It is one thing to act like a servant; it is another thing to be one. Jesus was simply a servant! A servant Christian is the freest person on earth. He chooses to serve. Regardless! He acts — not reacts. Servanthood is not weakness but incredible strength.

It Will Not Be So Among You

Read Mt. 20:20-28; Mk 9:33-37; 10:35-45; Luke 22:24-27. Read it again, closely, honestly. A crisis comes under the very shadow of the cross! Who is the greatest? Churches split over less issues! James and John (with their mother) want thrones? The remaining ten are angered over the fact they had not thought of that! Jesus had to be disappointed! After three years of intensified training they fail the test! Jesus counters, ". . . but it will not be so among

5

you". Power plays, politics, intimidation are foreign to the spirit of Christ. Servanthood never split a church; servanthood never hurt a church. Weak men tyrannize; strong men serve. The world may not understand many church doctrines; the world does understand service. Service cannot be denied.

The Mission Of The Church Is Submission

Read Eph. 3:21, 22. This one virtue solves all our problems. Even when we teach servanthood we forget submission. Submission is the foundation of servanthood. Submission is the mother of obedience. Obedience is far more than zealous activity. Many do only what they like to do. Others obey rules or strive to impress others. (Mt. 6). The spirit of obedience is to obey regardless. Submission is easier to talk about than to do. Human nature does not die easily.

All submit to someone. Even heaven's Trinity has subordination. The authority of Christ is rooted in the submission of Christ. This is the vital principle in Eph. 5:22-33. Some men conclude they are dictators; many women conclude they must be inferior. Submission is not inferiority. The church obeys Christ because Christ died for the church. Notice the subordinated are exhorted first in both Ephesians 5 and 6. When husbands love their wives like Christ did the church then wives joyously submit to them. This is poignant and powerful. Husbands, do yourself a favor, love your wives. Authority is not the first word in leadership — submission is. Only followers can qualify to become leaders. Paul said, "I am yours, to spend and be spent" (2 Cor. 12:14, 15). Leading is not lording (1 Pet. 5:1-3).

The Servant Church

The church was born on a cross and lives on a cross! Most know Luke 19:10 (to save the lost); but do we know Luke 22:27 (serve)? Jesus saved by serving. The church is here to serve the world; the world is not here to serve the church. The church is not won to win; the church is saved to serve. Many have taught without Biblical research that the work of the church is threefold — evangelism, edification, and benevolence. The work of the church is one — servanthood. To one who is lost the church serves that man by saving him. The attitude of evangelism is not "holier than thou". Evangelism is a servant of God knocking on a sinner's door to serve him humbly. Only servants scripturally evangelize. Don't send out the wrong people in evangelism. Saved people need taught. The church serves the saved by teaching them all things (Mt. 28:18-20). Bible classes are manned by servants. People in need are served in benevolence — without obligation!

6

The church that will not bleed cannot bless
The church that will not serve cannot save.
The church that will not suffer cannot redeem.
The church that will not die cannot live.

A Servant Pulpit

The crux of church ministry is deacons! "Deacon" means simply servant! Servant deacons become servant elders. The question is not, "Why don't more deacons become elders?" The question is, "Why don't more deacons become deacons?" Deacons who serve with wrong motives are not deacons! Who are deacons? Servants!

Read Mt. 25:21. Familiar passages must be read more closely! Notice the word — servant, not worker. A servant is a worker, but a worker may not be a servant! The compliment is to a servant, not a worker!

The pulpit of the church must be a servant pulpit! But what does this mean? This is crucial! Truth must be preached — but the attitude of truth must accompany the form! The speaker serves the audience. Many violate the truth by the way they present it. (Eph. 4:15). Ridicule has no place in the pulpit! To take advantage of people in a captive audience violates the Gospel! People did not hear the Gospel in such events — they merely saw our meanness! The Gospel is a form as well as a message, a spirit as well as a doctrine. The Gospel facts must be presented in a Gospel spirit.

Servant members, servant teachers, servant deacons, servant preachers, servant elders. Our prayer? "God, send me someone to serve". This is the heart of the matter. Jesus is "The Servant"; His church must be the "Church of the Servant".

Philip The Servant

Get out your Bibles! Perhaps the greatest revelation of servanthood is found with Philip.

ACTS 6 We are introduced to three primary men, Stephen, the first Christian martyr, Saul (Paul) the persecutor, and our hero, Philip, the servant. Saul stones Stephen. Stephen and Philip began as servants. They are the first two listed in the "seven". The only commodity God can use is a servant! God knows nothing else!

ACTS 8 Stephen is mourned; Saul makes havoc on the church; Philip, the servant, originates mission work! Where were the apostles? the Jerusalem church? Philip goes to Samaria. Philip was a "Hellenistic Jew" not local. Local Jews considered Samaritans as "dogs". No one was hated more than Samaritans! But Philip is a servant. Servants are "color-blind". Philip sought no prestigious pulpit — he simply sought to serve. Servants are used mightily by God. Many were baptized.

7

Then what happened? Simon the Sorceror was converted! Then Peter and John came? Did Philip resent this? No! He could have! Where were they when the "work" was done? But Philip realized they could give "apostolic hands". He proudly introduced them and took a "back seat". Why? Because he was a servant!

Then what happened? Was Philip invited to the A.C.U. Lectures? Did he make the "Church Circuit" telling how to baptize sinners? Did he write the official Church Growth book? *No!!!* God closed down the revival! What? Yes! Philip is sent to the boondocks! But he is happy! Servants are men under orders! They have no "axe-to-grind". If God wants him there he will be happy there. Servants go and do what they are told.

Then what happened? The Eunuch comes by in his wagon. Philip is told to "get into the chariot". Philip ran! Servants run! He used tact — "understandest thou what you readest?" He started in Isaiah 53 where the prospect was and preached unto him Jesus. Servants focus upon Jesus.

ACTS 21 This is powerful! The "proof of the pudding is in the eating". Christianity succeeds where all else fails! Philosophy does not talk about such; education cannot do it! Do what? Place Paul and Philip in the same house as beloved brethren. Paul and his group come to the house of Philip. Inspiration identifies this Philip as "one of the seven". This is Philip the servant! Agabus comes. He predicts pain if Paul goes to Jerusalem. Philip begs Paul not to go; Paul begs them not to cry! Paul and Philip, humanly speaking, should have been mortal enemies! Remember back in Acts 6? But Philip is a servant of Christ! Paul became a servant of Jesus Christ! In Christ all is resolved. This is the confession of a cross-bearer!

Questions

1. Does servanthood excite the ordinary man? Do we wish the sensational? the spectacular? What is the mind of Christ?

2. Perhaps a towel can be brought to class. Dramatize the towel in John 13 as you will. Are you secured? Discuss the difference between choosing to serve and simply being a servant.

3. Discuss in depth, "It will not be so among you".

4. Have you ever heard a class lesson, pulpit sermon on "Submission". How/why have we missed this? Discuss Ephesians 5:22–23. What is the first word in leadership?

5. Discuss the "Servant Church". What is the *ONE* real work of the church?

6. Discuss a "Servant Pulpit". We have the truth — but do we have the proper attitude. What is our prayer?

7. Take time and cover the life and times of Philip.

Chapter Three

I Love You

The Bible is one big collection of love letters God has sent his children. His message is clear — "I Love You!" (John 3:16) Not only did this message come on paper, it also came in the flesh—God's living Word-Jesus Christ! (1 John 1:1-2) Yes, God loved us so much that while we were yet dead in our sins He sent his only begotten Son to give his life for us so that we might have the hope of everlasting life!! That's love! That is God saying in a most profound way . . . "I Love You." Christians today are to be people overflowing with this same kind of love. Agape love. That is the subject of this chapter.

We followers of Christ appreciate God's love for us. As matter of fact only a true believer can even begin to grasp its depth! It is foolishness to the world.

While standing in the shadows of the cross, Jesus said these words.

> "A new commandment I give unto you, That ye love one another; as I have loved you, that ye also love one another. By this shall all men know that ye are my disciples, if ye have love one to another."
> (John 13:34-35)

This kind of love is taught to us by God. (I Thess. 4:9) It is mentioned throughout the New Testament as an identifying mark of a true believer. It is a fruit of the Spirit. (Gal. 5:22) that grows as we mature in the Lord. This love is our primary motivation for serving the risen Christ for it is the same love that caused God to offer his only Son in our behalf!

Love Letters

In 2 Cor. 2:4 Paul referring to an earlier letter written to the Christians there states:

"That ye might know the love which I have more abundantly unto you." Paul was saying, "I love you" and "its growing". Interestingly, he is writing to perhaps the most selfish, immature church in existence at that time. This is another proof that he possessed the kind of love (agape) that Jesus had commanded his disciples to have. It was a love that didn't depend on circumstances or conditions. It wasn't a "I'll love you if" kind of love. It was a sacrificial, dying to self, a lifting of others attitude. 1 Corinthians 13 reminds us that we may do all sorts of wonderful Christian works, even possess a mountain moving faith . . . but if we accomplish these without love it adds up to one big zero! It is nothing! What a lesson to be learned in the Kingdom of God today!

Sealed With The Spirit

That Bible is God's Book of love. Jesus in the flesh was a living love letter. (John 1:1, 1 John 1:1-2) The apostles took on this same image. (2 Cor. 2:14-3:3) As disciples of Christ today and followers of the apostles' inspired writings we too are to become living love letters of the Kingdom. (2 Cor. 3; 1 Cor. 11:1) We are letters that are instruments of God; we are sealed with the Holy Spirit. (2 Cor.1:21-22; 5:5; Eph. 1:13-14) Not only does this guarantee us our inheritance, it also empowers us to be increasing in its glory. (2 Cor.3:17-18) As this happens we find our love increasing (abounding) and spreading to others. (1 Thess. 4:9-10) Others in the world are "reading" us — and the message is to be as clear as God's was on the cross . . . " I LOVE YOU!!"

Perfumed Letters

Remember when you were dating and received perfumed letters from your loved one? Even before the letter was opened you knew it was from someone who was special . . . someone who really cared about you. The message of the perfume said, "I love you".

This is exactly the way a Christian's life and the word of God work together! Explore 2 Cor. 1-3 again. Especially notice the following:

> "Now thanks be to God, which always causeth us to triumph in Christ, and maketh manifest the savour of his knowledge by us in every place. For we are unto God a sweet savour (aroma or fragrance) of Christ, in them that are saved, and in them that perish: to the one we are the savour of death unto death; and to the other the savour of life unto life. And who is sufficient for these things? For we are not as many, which corrupt the word of God; but as of sincerity, but as of God, in the sight of God speak we in Christ."
>
> (2 Cor. 2:14-17)

The World (others) know we are Christ's disciples by our love -our actions - even before we share the actual word with them! The Word is the power of God unto salvation. (Romans 1:16; 1 Cor. 1:18) And it is only through the word that we can be saved - the preaching of the gospel. But, if we share the word with others and do not do it with a spirit of love . . . it will accomplish nothing. (1 Cor. 13:1ff) It is only when we become living love letters - when we have the word "written on our hearts" and share this word in love, that we will see the fruit that God intends for us to witness!! When combined, we have the most powerful, attractive, life-changing, soul-saving instrument in the universe. As a matter of fact . . . the only one!! Our message may smell like death to some; but to those who want real life, our message smells like "the aroma of life"!! (2 Cor. 2:16) We might ask ourselves . . . what do we smell like? What are our friends and neighbors smelling? Is our life style making "corrupt the word"? We are to be perfumed letters!!

You Can't Have One Without The Other
The message from Paul is only an expansion of Jesus' teaching.

> " . . . Thou shalt love the Lord thy God with all thy heart, and with all thy soul, and with all thy mind. This is the first and great commandment. And the second is like unto it, Thou shalt love thy neighbor as thyself. On these two commandments hang all the law and the prophets."
>
> (Matthew 22:37–40)

Throughout all history this has been God's great command. Read 1 John 3:14–4:21; and 5:2–3.

In John's letter we find the same challenge of Jesus' command and Paul's teaching. Here we find the source of being this kind of love letter and we also see some problems associated with not loving as we should.

We can't love others until we love God! Perhaps this is why we have so many in our churches today who do not know how to love one another; they never learned to love God because they have never really discovered God's love for them! God loved us first. He sent His Son to be the propitiation for our sins . . . and because we recognize, believe and teach this fact . . . we love one another! (1 John 4:10–11) When we love one another God abides in us and his love is perfected in us. This is in obedience to His commandments.

The person who doesn't constantly reflect back on the cross and all the love, mercy and grace that was manifested there is not able to love others! The Christian who doesn't share his love with others cannot love God! You can't have one without the other! A person may say they love God yet not be concerned about their brothers. God says that person is a liar! (1 John 4:20) Perhaps the diagrams below will help us to see this more clearly.

	God			God			God	
Others	O O	Self	Others	O←O	Self	Others	O⇄O	Self

Stage 1 love	Stage 2 love	Stage 3 love
I realize God's love for me and others. I am still selfish, obedient.	(perfected love) Now I show love to others. By this obedience I also manifest my love to God. I obey his commandments.	(Fruition) Others know I love them and they also share this love with God and others.

11

Loving others is a growing process. How do we know we are maturing in this kind of love? One good way is to observe how often we actually tell others in a verbal way. A disciple shouldn't have any problem communicating the same thing Jesus told him! When is the last time you looked a brother or sister in the eyes and said, "I love you?"

Conclusion

Let us love others as Christ loved us!
Let us love others and treat others as we want to be treated!
Let us obey the commandments of the Lord!
Let us verbally tell others . . . "I Love You."

Questions

1. If a nonbeliever "read" me as a living love letter they would describe my life as . . .
2. Why would some profess to love God yet not love their brothers?
3. Reviewing the three stages of love, I'd have to say I am in stage #_____. How am I going to improve this? When am I going to start?
4. 1 Cor. 13 teaches that I may do all sorts of wonderful Christian works but if these are not done in love they add up to _____.
5. List ten practical ways you can tell others "I love You".

Chapter Four

All I Am And All I Have Is By The Grace Of God

"But by the grace of God I am what I am: and his grace which was bestowed upon me was not in vain; but I laboured more abundantly than they all: yet not I, but the grace of God which was with me."

1 Cor. 15:10

Amazing grace, how sweet the sound!
That saved a wretch like me!
I once was lost, but now am found;
Was blind, but now I see.

Introduction

GRACE!!! Discipleship begins, continues, and ends by grace! "For by grace are ye saved through faith; and that not of yourselves: it is the gift of God: not of works, lest any man should boast. For we are his workmanship, created in Christ Jesus unto good works, which God hath before ordained that we should walk in them" (Eph. 2:8-10). Memorize this, "The only permanent motivation in Christianity is grace". People call enthusiasts regularly suggesting, "Motivate us!" This contagion pumps one up temporarily only to let him down. Frustration, failure, cynicism results! The soil both of salvation and service is grace. Unbelievable, amazing, too-good-to-be-true grace!

The Gospel Of Grace

Tell men what God did before you tell them what to do! The Gospel is what God did for man at the cross. The Gospel is not the conditions of response. "But none of these things move me, neither count I my life dear unto myself, so that I might finish my course with joy, and the ministry, which I have received of the Lord Jesus, to testify the gospel of the grace of God" (Acts 20:24). Salvation is not a business transaction. A deal was not struck with God — heaven pays fifty cents and man fifty cents. We didn't "shake hands" on the deal. Grace is God's initiative, God's product! "Jesus paid it all". One hundred cents on the dollar. Man pays nothing — not even the interest — he does not even "get the tip" for a free meal. To God be the glory. Man accepts what God did! Man does not buy, earn, merit, deserve grace! Earned grace would cease being grace! Man does not qualify for grace — the grace is there! Grace qualified for has ceased being grace.

The Gospel (Good News) is God's power to save (Rom. 1:16, 17). Grace demands works but works have no place for grace! One "obeys the Gospel, not law" (Rom. 6:17, 18; 2 Thess. 1:7–9). Don't turn the "Good News" into "Bad News". Evangelism, the Great Commission, is telling sinners what God did (Mt. 28:18–20; Mk. 16:15, 16). Paul confronted and smote men with the cross (Gal. 6:14; 1 Cor. 2:1–5; 15:1–4). Sinners are not motivated to repent by the badness of men but by the goodness of God (Rom. 2:4; 2 Cor. 7:9, 10).

Turn and read Galatians 1. The Galatians saved by the Gospel are now seeking another. Think! Paul is not saying that there is another doctrine — he said "another gospel". The Galatian was leaving grace for man-made works. His "gospel" was what man knew and did rather than the genuine Gospel — what God did! Preach Christ. Christ obeyed results in the church (Acts 2:41–47). Concentrate in Matthew, Mark, Luke, and John. These accounts focus upon Jesus. The power is Jesus; the glory is to God. Plant the accounts and you reap Acts. You do not plant Acts to reap Acts. The Gospel is the Savior! Preach the Savior! The law confronts man with his own strength and asks him to use it to his limit; the Gospel places man before the Gift of God and asks him to use/live what God has provided (2 Cor. 9:15; Col. 3:1–4). Remember! The power to live the epistles is found in the gospels! It is the grace of God which restores life, which takes human nature unto His service and gives it a place in the kingdom.

Charis

The poignant Greek word for grace is "charis". It is the root word for joy, pleasure, loveliness! Favor felt produces gratitude. Grace cannot be deserved; it is the unmerited love of God. Someone observed:

> Justice: We get what we deserve
> Mercy: We do not get what we deserve
> Grace: We get what we do not deserve

GRACE!!! Grace is positive acceptance in spite of the other person; a demonstration of love that is unearned, undeserved; and unpayable. Man cannot save himself by himself. Grace gives God all the glory; there is nothing in which man can boast (Rom. 3:24–31; 4:1–5; 11:6). This makes grace to some a stumbling block. Man wishes to be self-sufficient! Pride dies hard. Man's question remains, "Isn't there something I can do?" Tragically those who need grace the most have the greatest difficulty in accepting it! One does not perform to be accepted — being accepted one performs.

Grace is the "pantry" of all God's blessings — love, joy, peace, wisdom, strength, etc. This is the reservoir of all that God has. Grace is a gift; a gift is to be received, treasured, and used. It is "free gratis". We are saved by grace; don't ever forget it.

Grace Demands Works

Grace is not universalism! God will not save those who do not wish to be. Coerced grace would not be grace. Salvation will never be "crammed down throats". God is at the mercy of man's acceptance. Wrath does not result in grace but grace demands wrath! *RE-READ OUR TEXT!!* Grace does more. God's work cannot be done by human strength! The grace within works without. Our "works failure" is a "grace failure". Paul was given a thorn in 2 Corinthians 12 to enforce 2 Cor. 5:14, "For the love of Christ constraineth (compels, motivates) us." It is not our love for God but His love for us. Every morning awaken with two thoughts — God loves me and Christ died for me! My love for God is determined by my acceptance of His! *REMEMBER!!* The only permanent motivation in Christianity is grace! "And he said unto me, my grace is sufficient for thee: for my strength is made perfect in weakness. Most gladly therefore will I rather glory in my infirmities, that the power of Christ may rest upon me." (2 Cor. 12:9).

> I cannot work my soul to save
> That work my Lord has done.
> But I will work like any slave
> For the love of God's dear Son!

Perhaps our singing has been deeper than our preaching!

> O love that will not let me go
> I give Thee back the life I owe.

Grace is no "blue-eyed blond". It is no "cop-out" of ease. Grace is the most demanding thing on earth. It is a "disgrace" not to accept grace! I am crucified with Christ; nevertheless I live; yet not I, but Christ liveth in me: and the life which I now live in the flesh I live by faith of the Son of God, who loved me, and gave himself for me. I do not frustrate the grace of God: for if righteousness come by the law, then Christ is dead in vain" (Gal. 2:20, 21). "We then, as workers together with him, beseech you also that ye receive not the grace of God in vain" (2 Cor. 6:1). One may be wrong about some things but he cannot be wrong about grace!

Falling From Grace

Grace does not advocate "once saved always saved" . . . the inability of apostasy. "Christ is become of no effect unto you, whosoever of you are justified by the law; ye are fallen from grace" (Gal. 5:4). The Bible says Christians can fall! *ANY MAN, ANYWHERE CAN GO TO HELL! REMEMBER!* Familiar scriptures must be read more closely. Fallen Christians fall from

GRACE — not law, works, the church! We are saved by grace and kept by grace. Too many preach Christianity as "Saved by grace then kept by law". The shout is "more, more, more". Christianity is not religious humanism. God does not drop a "black book out of the sky (the Bible)" saying, "Good Luck". Legalism fails! Legalism results in guilt and fear. Don't preach guilt without grace! Legalism fears that something we still do not know and that something we should have done. There can be no security in merited works. Security is located in grace; our faith is in Him not us; our works are His works. The Jews stumbled over grace — why? Because grace cut the taproot of their arrogance in self-justification (1 Cor. 1:17-26). In Matthew 19 the Rich Young Ruler walked away from grace seeking works. God is able to make us able (2 Cor. 9:6-8). We receive "more grace" (James 4:6). Peter concludes his ministry, "But grow in grace, and in the knowledge of our Lord and Saviour Jesus Christ. To him be glory both now and forever. Amen" (2 Pet. 3:18).

Someone said the most profound thought is, "Jesus Loves Me"; the most simple thought, "Jesus is Lord". Our text is not as interested in "falling from grace" as "standing in grace". The answer to "falling" is "standing". If you can know you are fallen you can equally know you are standing! One must accept Christ as a gift before He will follow Him as an example (1 Pet. 5:12).

Grace makes one gracious. Our "mercy problem" is actually a "grace problem". People who will not accept grace cannot give mercy. Grace received produces mercy. God is gracious (1 Pet. 2:3); His people must be gracious.

God Is More Than His Gifts

A modern thought is blasphemous, "Do your *BEST* and God will do the *REST!*" God does it all! Without Him we are nothing (John 15:1-10). God works (the energy) in us working out our salvation (Phil. 2:12, 13).

Yet grace is more than gifts! Grace is God! God is grace! "But the God of all grace, who hath called us unto his eternal glory by Christ Jesus, after that ye have suffered a while, make you perfect, stablish, strengthen, settle you" (1 Pet. 5:10). Christians do not merely want from God — they want God. We do not merely want salvation from God but God-our-salvation! The ultimate happiness is not merely having His gifts but *HIM!* God's grace (gift) is complete — the greatest gift is God Himself!

> O Lord, give me grace to feel the need of thy grace.
> Give me grace to ask for thy grace
> And when in thy grace thou hast given me
> Grace — give me the grace to use thy grace.
> Duchess of Gordon

Questions

1. *GRACE!* Are we ready to study grace? Will we wrestle with the profound depths of grace? Do we covet grace? Can we really accept pure grace?
2. Discuss preaching what God did before telling men what to do. Discuss the meaning of grace.
3. Were you motivated by the goodness of God or your badness? Discuss Galatians 1. Do you focus upon Matthew, Mark, Luke, and John?
Have we preached the Saviour?
4. Discuss how man's pride stumbles over grace.
5. Discuss how grace demands/motivates works. Does one work to get grace or because of grace?
6. What is the only permanent motivation in Christianity?
7. Discuss "Falling From Grace". Are we saved by grace then kept by law? Where is the security?
8. Discuss graciousness. Discuss "Do your best and God will do the rest".

Chapter Five

I Believe

"Jesus said unto him, If thou canst believe, all things are possible to him that believeth.
And straightway the father of the child cried out, and said with tears, Lord, I believe; help thou mine unbelief."

Mark 9:23, 24

"For thee which I also suffer these things: nevertheless I am not ashamed: for I know whom I have believed, and am persuaded that he is able to keep that which I have committed unto him against that day."

2 Timothy 1:12

Introduction

FAITH! Christianity is a system of faith. Disciples are believers; even more disciples are believers in Christ. Disciples confess daily, "Jesus is Lord". This is their creed and life. Faith is one familiar, used term. But what, actually, is meant by faith? You will hear a zillion answers. All think they have faith; all think they understand faith. All are so sure about their faith. Faith that is sure of itself is not faith. Faith that is sure about God is the only faith there is.

Satan has had a "field day" over faith. To some works (deeds) is more important than faith. Others, reacting to meritorious works, demand a "faith only apart from works". Faith without works is absurd (James 2); the old English was quite on target — belief was bylief. How one actually lives is, in reality, what one really believes. He may not know it — he may even deny it — but faith and life are synonymous. Moderns try to arrive at fellowship via deeds (activities); scripture arrives at fellowship via faith (Acts 2:42). Believe and you will belong; you may outwardly belong yet not believe.

Faith is not magic. Notice these familiar phrases, "I wish I had your faith", "I wish I had more faith", "If only I had more faith," "My faith has not lived up to its expectations". Such reduces faith to human effort, to self. This reduces faith to religious positive thinking. It is my stamina, knowledge, works. Therefore many believe in believing. "It doesn't make any difference what you believe as long as you are honest and sincere". The object of such faith is self! How absurd! Faith is not a magic wand waved over life to iron out the creases.

Habakkuk said, ". . . but the just shall live by his faith" (Hab. 2:4). This is quoted in the New Testament (Rom. 1:17; Gal. 3:11; Heb. 10:38). Throughout history man has been saved by faith. Perhaps a better translation, "by faith the just live". Faith is not in faith — faith is in its object. This is crucial. Faith is in its object! To illustrate. One huge bulldozer was mired in mud. Another big bulldozer was brought to pull it out. Would a string suffice? a rope? a small chain? *NO!* All the believing on earth could not enable something weak to do such a job! Then one huge railroad chain is hooked up! It is strong enough to do the job. So you use the chain and the work is done. Believing or not believing does not change the strength of the chain! Our faith does not make God stronger; our lack of faith does not make Him weaker! Our faith in God will determine how much we utilize Him! The Christian faith is in its object — Christ. Our faith is not in our own knowledge, works, lives. Our faith is in Him!

Again, faith is not a business transaction. Too many reduce salvation to a business deal. "God, you do that and I will do this". God pays 50¢ and man pays 50¢ *BLASPHEMY!* Jesus paid it all! Faith accepts what God did! Faith applies what God provides. Faith is a system; law is a system. Law is something man keeps; faith is something man has in God. Years ago Melancthon said, "It is faith alone, which saves, but the faith that saves is not alone". Only through faith can Christ be accepted. Disciples know in whom they have believed.

Grace Through Faith

Man is saved by grace (Eph. 2:5-10). We are saved by atonement and not attainment. "To declare, I say, at this time his righteousness: that he might be just, and the justifier of him which believeth in Jesus. Where is the boasting then. It is excluded. By what law? of works? Nay: but by the law of faith" (Rom. 3:26, 27). "Now to him that worketh is the reward not reckoned of grace, but of debt. But to him that worketh not, but believeth on him that justifieth the ungodly, his faith is counted for righteousness" (Rom. 4:4, 5). "And if by grace, then it is no more of works; otherwise grace is no more grace. But if it be of works, then it is no more grace: otherwise work is no more work" (Rom. 1:6). If grace is not for sinners it is not grace (Rom. 5:5-8). If mercy is not for the undeserving, it is no longer mercy (Mt. 9:13). To boast about faith is senseless. It renders man both bankrupt and helpless. Faith is surrender; faith is total dependence. Faith is the end of one's boasting! Faith lives by grace — not works; it does not achieve but receive. A man may go to heaven — without health, without wealth, without fame, without a great name, without learning, without big earnings, without culture, without friends, without a thousand other things — but not *WITHOUT CHRIST!* ". . . and this is the victory that overcometh the world, even our faith" (1 John 5:4).

Salvation is a gift (Rom. 6:23; Eph. 2:8-10; 2 Cor. 9:15). A gift is received by faith. The Gospel believers hear/believe is about Christ. Repentance is caused by Christ. The confession is Christ. Baptism into Christ puts on Christ (Rom. 6:3, 4; Gal. 3:26, 27).

Our life is in Christ (Col. 3:1-4). To be in Christ makes you fit for heaven; Christ in you makes you fit for earth. To a disciple Christ is our home address. *CHRIST-CHRIST-CHRIST!* Consequently faith is the most decisive thing in Christianity. Not a *SPECIAL* faith but a *SIMPLE* faith. Faith does not change circumstances; faith changes us. Man cannot be saved by a perfect obedience because he cannot render it. He cannot be saved by imperfect obedience because God cannot accept it. The only solution is God's gift — *CALVARY!* Faith is a daring, living, casting of self upon God's grace (Col. 2:6). Let faith be faith; let Jesus Christ be our faith. Faith by its very nature is something/someone lived. The Gospel of God proclaims, "You belong to me". Faith answers, "I belong to you". The only appropriate response to grace is faith. Faith casts itself upon God. Martin Luther said, "The evidence of our faith is the acceptance of grace."

Faith And Obedience

In order to receive grace man must believe it; in order to enjoy grace man must obey it! Obedience is the response of faith to the grace of God. "For by grace are ye saved through faith; and that not of yourselves: it is the gift of God: not of works, lest any man should boast. For we are his workmanship, created in Christ Jesus unto good works, which God hath before ordained that we should walk in them" (Eph. 2:8, 10). ". . . work out your own salvation with fear and trembling. For it is God which worketh in you both to will and to do of his good pleasure" (Phil. 2:12, 13). The only permanent motivation in Christianity is grace! (1 Cor. 15:10; 2 Cor. 5:14). Faith obeys the grace of God! Faith is like a muscle — it must be exercised. Faith is like a sunrise — it must arise fresh every morning. Man is not saved by grace then kept by law. The faith that keeps is the same as the faith that saves. Faith allows one to be kept by the power of God. "Who are kept by the power of God through faith unto salvation ready to be revealed in the last time" (1 Pet. 1:5). There cannot be saving/living faith apart from obedience: We cannot be protected against ourselves in spite of ourselves.

Do not confuse obedience with merit. Merit, not obedience, cancels grace. Merit means to earn by performance; obedience is faith in action. One's faith is solely in Christ — not our conversion, not an experience. Allow nothing to substitute itself for Christ. Another distinction should be observed — one has an obedience of faith not merely faith in obedience. ". . . for obedience to the faith among all nations, for his name" (Rom. 1:5). "But now is made manifest, and by the scriptures of the prophets, according to the commandment of the everlasting God, made known to all nations for the obedience of faith!" (Rom. 16:26).

Finish

Faith is not for an instant; faith if for life. Moderns are known for "starting" but not "finishing". *IT IS ALWAYS TOO SOON TO QUIT!* Life is decided by faith. "The just shall live by faith" Christianity cannot be reduced to a new birth; it is a new life.

"... be thou faithful unto death, and I will give thee a crown of life" (Rev. 2:10). Familiar scriptures must be read more closely. To be faithful is to be full of faith. Faithfulness is not neurotic activities. Keep your faith and your faith will keep you. Believe and keep believing. Faith is not will power, it is Christ power. Disciples are not trying to "hold on for dear life"; they are holding on to the Faithful One!

Back to Rev. 2:10. The word translated "unto" is actually "until". Check it out. *FINISH!* Start then finish. Keep on keeping on in faith. "But none of these things moved me, neither count I my life dear unto myself, so that I might finish my cause with joy, and the ministry, which I have received of the Lord Jesus, to testify the gospel of the grace of God" (Acts 20:24).

The Wheelbarrow

A balancing act featured a man pushing a wheelbarrow across a high wire. He loaded the wheelbarrow and did it. Then he did it blindfolded. He then asked the audience, "Do you believe in my ability?" They all said, "Yes". He then countered, "Get into the wheelbarrow". Disciples are people in God's wheelbarrow.

Questions

1. Discuss the various misconcepts of faith. Should one re-evaluate our own thinking/teaching? Discuss the merit of faith as it focuses upon its object.
2. Discuss Habakkuk 2:4. Discuss the "chain" illustration.
3. Have we reduced salvation to a business transaction? Did Jesus stamp, "Paid in Full"? Discuss salvation as a gift.
4. Discuss "grace and faith" versus "law and works".
5. Discuss faith and obedience . . . the difference between obedience and merit.
   Wherein does faith boast?
6. Discuss the enduring quality of faith . . . *FINISH*. Discuss the "Wheelbarrow Story".

Chapter Six

I Am Afraid

We've all experienced it . . . a phone call in the middle of the night and a broken, shakey voice on the other end replies . . . "I'm afraid I have some bad news for you." Fear races through our being! An accident? . . . heart attack? . . . a burnout? . . . loss of job. . . or even death? All humans are subject to fear. Wrestling with fear is an every day challenge for the disciple of Christ. We know the word teaches that we are not to be fearful, but no one seems to escape its grip at times.

What is a healthy, honest, scriptural view of fear? How is a Cross-bearer to cope with its threat? In this chapter we want to explore fear by studying Job's encounter with what most of us would consider a disaster.

"Painful agony in the presence or anticipation of danger" is perhaps the best description of what we think of as fear. If it appears suddenly we think of it as panic or terror. Adam, Isaac, Moses, Elijah, David, Mary and the apostles are famous examples of Godly people who experienced fear. Job is a classic example. God's word describes him as "perfect and upright, and one that feared God, and shunned evil". (1:1) "the greatest of all the men of the East." (1:3) He worshipped God continually. (1:5). He had been richly blessed. (1:10) "A man of integrity." (2:3) So we are talking about a God-fearing, family man. Today we would call him a "mature", "faithful", or "committed Christian".

As we read further concerning Job we discover that although he had this wonderful relationship with the Lord, he had also feared disaster might come upon him:

> "For the thing I *greatly feared* is come upon me, and that which *I was afraid* is come unto me." (3:25)

The remainder of the book deals with a man of God wrestling with God's will and coming out victorious in the end.

It's interesting to note that Job's fears centered around the same things that we fear today:

1. The fear of losing material possessions. (1:9–17)
2. The fear of harm or death of family members or loved ones. (1:18–19)
3. The fear of personal pain or death. (2:7–10)

The world bases its faith and measures its success in *things, good health,* and *"looking out for Number One."* Fear of losing one or all of these is perhaps the most prevalent emotion in today's world.

All of the fears we have were learned except those of falling and the fear of loud noises . . . we were born with those. Every Christian struggles with fear. Many fears are conquered . . . but world-wide still remains one of the leading causes of physical and mental problems.

In this chapter we want to examine the three areas of fear mentioned above and see what God teaches concerning them.

Things

Possessions have become God to many people today! We are living in a world bombarded by advertising and peers telling us all the *things* we need in order to be happy and successful. Our society is trying to find security in possessions. Jesus said long ago:

> "take heed, and beware of covetousness: for a man's life consisteth not in the abundance of the things which he possesseth."
>
> (Luke 12:15)

He also affirms in Matthew 6:33 that if we seek His Kingdom first all these things will be taken care of! Do we believe this? Then why are so many . . . yes, even Christian people falling into materialism? There isn't anything wrong with possessions as long as they are holy and being used by us in a rightful manner. They also must take a lower priority in our hearts then God. Job had possessions, but they did not possess him!! As in Job's case, Satan is always trying to destroy a person's faith any way he can! Satan's first attack was on Job's possessions.

Examine Philippians Chapter 2. As we become more "like minded" with Jesus and other Christians, *things* begin to be over shadowed with the more important aspects of one's spiritual life. We become more concerned about others having things for example, than ourselves. (2:4) Paul goes on to state in Philippians 3:7-8.

> "But what *things* were gain to me, those I counted loss for Christ. Yea doubtless, and I count all *things* but loss for the excellency of the knowledge of Christ Jesus my Lord: for whom I have suffered the loss of all *things,* and do count them but dung that I may win Christ . . ."

There is nothing wrong in a Christian having many material blessings, but these must be secondary to winning Christ. This attitude quickly removes much of our fears concerning losing things.

A friend of mine recently died from cancer. During the last year of his life he often expressed to me that *things* didn't seem as important anymore. His main concern was his personal relationship with the Lord and the welfare of his family. He could relate with Job:

> "naked I came out of my mother's womb, and naked shall I return thither: the Lord gave, and the Lord taketh away; blessed be the name of the Lord."
>
> (Job 1:21)

The disciple of Jesus Christ is storing up treasure in heaven, not on the earth. (Matthew 19:21) Lets be careful that we don't let things of this world keep us in a fearful state. That would be sin.

Harm Or Loss Of Loved Ones

Few things strike us as hard as the harm or loss of a family member or close loved one. Job's children were precious to him as ours are to us. The very thought of disease, injury or death coming to them can create fear with in us. Satan's second attack was on Job's children. This shows just how vicious Satan is!

God wants us healthy. (2 John 2; James 5:16) He wants to have life to the full. (John 10:10) Death of loved ones brought tears to the eyes of Jesus. (John 11:35) Yet, God's will isn't always our will. Job suffered. He and other Bible greats suffered and even wished they could die at times. God did not remove Paul's thorn in the flesh. Neither are we relieved of the pain and death that surrounds us. These things should simply bring us into more dependence in God. Our faith grows stronger out of sorrow and tribulation. (James 1:1-6) Death to the Christian is viewed as a graduation to glory! It isn't the end. It is the door way to a greater existence. (1 Thess. 4:13-18) This passage ends by encouraging us to ". . . comfort one another with these words." Inordinate fear of death is slavery! The Hebrew writer states:

> "who through fear of death were all their life time subject to bondage."
>
> (Hebrews 2:15)

A person who is not absorbed in a strong devotional life; in prayer and the word, can be destroyed by the death of a loved one! We may question God as did Job: "why was I even born?" Yet, we know everything will work out for good. (Romans 8:28)

My wife and I lost our first child two days after birth. For the first day no one knew anything was wrong with the baby. What a joy to see my wife nurse and care for our bundle of love. The grandparents were thrilled. The third day she was dead! Why? How could this happen to us? What good could ever come from our loss? Yet, now fifteen years later we have been able to counsel and comfort dozens of other couples who have lost children. Romans 8:28 has a much clearer meaning for us now.

25

The Fear Of Personal Pain Or Death

Satan's third attack was on Job's body. (Job 2:7-10) Man feels threatened! Witness the many survival movements in this nation today. Stockpiles of weapons, food and shelters are springing up all across the nation. By nature, man is a survivalist and I suppose if there ever is a nuclear war, man will survive. We are extremely concerned about our health and environment. We jog and watch our food. We are safety conscience. But God isn't so concerned about our physical fitness and our security as He is with our doing His will!! He is concerned that we live and die "in the Lord!"

"Ye shall know the truth and the truth shall make you free." (John 8:32) In many ways Paul was the Job of the New Testament. He had conquered the fear of death and was ready to be delivered. His beautiful words at the end of 2 Timothy should comfort us in our personal illness and even in death. Death to the Christian is a victory. (1 Cor. 15) If we believe God's word, we can face our own death with courage!!

Conclusion

The one great fear we should have is not that of losing things, others or self, but the fear of losing our souls. A Reverent fear of God can lead us unto salvation. His is the one to be feared. (Proverbs 1:7 and Eccl. 12:13) Some fear is good. God gave us a natural fear for our protection. Yet, Satan can magnify these fears into monsters that can destroy us instead of helping. He is the source of death and destruction. (Job 1; Genesis 3) He enslaves people with the fears described in this lesson. He is to be feared himself. (Luke 12:5) The inordinate fears he creates in us can damn us eternally. (Rev. 21:8) This knowledge should also bring us closer to the Lord. We need God's help and he promises to be there. We also need daily encouragement from fellow believers. (Heb. 3:13) We must have hope and faith in God. We must believe that he is able to see us through. He is able to empower us to overcome. (Eph. 3:16) All things will work out to our good. (Romans 8:28)

> When the shepherds were afraid, God's answer was "Fear not." (Luke 2)
> When the disciples were afraid, God's answer was "Fear not." (John 6)
> When we are threatened, we can answer, "I will not fear" (Hebrews 13:6)

Man will always have fears, but these can be tamed by Jesus. Only God can give us a spirit of discernment which enables us to know what and whom to fear. This can only come from a deep, abiding relationship with Christ.

In the end, Job was blessed with more than he had in the beginning. (Job 42) Satan was the loser! Praise God! The God of love made sure his man was a winner! That can also be true of us.

> "There is no fear in love; but perfect love casteth out fear: because fear hath torment. He that feareth is not made perfect in love."
>
> (1 John 4:18)

Questions
1. Man is born with only two fears _____ and _____.
   Where do we get the rest?
2. Name some natural fears that God has given us for our protection.
3. How can Satan turn these "good" fears into destructive ones?
4. In what ways do we fear the same things as Job?
5. List some practical ways we can overcome fear. Discuss.

Chapter Seven

I Am Thankful

Disciples are to be people of humble thanksgiving. We are to show gratitude to God and to others for the blessings we enjoy. One little boy was overheard praying:

> "I thank you for those I like and for those I don't like;
> I thank you for what I have and for what I don't have!"

This is precisely the attitude Jesus challenges us to have! From one of His experiences we will study how we can meet this challenge.

Where Are The Nine?

Once Jesus healed ten men who were lepers. (Read Luke 17:11-19) Leprosy was one of the most feared diseases of mankind in that day. In some ways it was worse than our present day cancer. It deformed, maimed and killed its victims. Imagine having this terrible disease and then one day bumping into the great physician who could completely heal all manner of illness, even raise the dead from the grave! With some blind, some missing limbs, faces scarred, dying a slow, cruel death they began to warn Jesus' company with shouts of "Unclean, unclean!" This was the custom of the day. Recognizing Jesus — the man of compassion (John 11:35) — the one who touched and healed other lepers (Luke 5:13) they began to shout again — "Jesus, Master, have mercy on us." The Bible says "When He saw them, He said unto them, go show yourselves unto the priests." (verse 14) The ten lepers did what Jesus commanded and while on their way to the priests — "AS THEY WALKED" — they were immediately healed! Then the shocker! — only one of the ten returned to thank Jesus! Jesus, perhaps with wonder written across His face, asked:

> "Were there not ten cleansed: but WHERE ARE THE NINE?" (verse 17)

The healer then turned his complete attention to the grateful one and spoke words we should all remember.

> "Arise, go thy way: thy faith hath made thee whole." (verse 19)

Jesus only complimented the one who said "Thank you." Christians have so much to be thankful for. Do we thank God for all the good things or do we practice what has been called "the respectable sin" — Ingratitude? Let's examine some specific things for which we should be grateful.

Thankful For Being Alive

First, Christians are to be thankful for being alive! God created each of us as individuals and for a purpose. He knew us in our mother's womb. (Jer. 1), He has plans for our lives (Eph. 1), and has given us gifts to be used. (1 Pet. 4:10) He has even made an appointment for our death (Heb. 9:27). God's people are to carefully be "redeeming the time" (Eph. 5:16).

One man prayed daily, "I thank you for being alive today, please help me make the world a better place." Christians need to pray that prayer. We need to be thankful for the life God has given us to live and testify for Him. God not only gives us life, but life "to the full". Our "cup runneth over". Are we grateful?

When people come to me depressed and bored with living, I simply send them immediately to visit the hospital (especially the emergency and ICU waiting rooms) or to the local nursing home. There they are to help someone. Usually within an hour they are feeling better about their own life!

When the leper realized he was cured, he was thankful for life. Let's be thankful we are alive to serve God!

Thankful For Salvation

Jesus was moved because the nine he healed from disease were ungrateful. Can you imagine how He must anguish over those he died for on Calvary who turn their backs on Him!? Like the lepers, we all were dead in our sins! (Romans 5:8) We had no hope. We were on our way to a devil's hell when Christ stepped in and became a sacrifice for us. He gave us life (Eph. 2; Col. 2:13)

> "And He is the propitiation for our sins: and not for ours only, but also for the sins of the whole world."
>
> (1 John 2:2)

Do we really appreciate that? If we aren't thankful for the cross, we will never show God any real gratitude for anything else! The cross must cast a shadow over all that we have and all that we do.

> "But thanks be to God, which giveth us the victory through our Lord Jesus Christ." (I Cor. 15:57) "Thanks be to God for His unspeakable gift." (II Cor. 9:15)

> "But God be thanked, that ye were the servants of sin, but ye have obeyed from the heart that form of doctrine which was delivered you." (Romans 6:17)

Just think what all the nine missed in Luke 17. They were not

30

totally healed — just bodily. Spiritually, perhaps became worse off! With a "cleansed" body and no righteousness they could indulge in more sin than before! Ungrateful people are some of the most unhappy and ungodly in the world. The nine probably went on to make up for lost time — getting all the "gusto" while they could!

Disciples of Jesus Christ must appreciate salvation. Without salvation life would be an awful, depressing venture.

Someone has said "If Jesus had not come, Satan would have already turned this world into hell!" Can we even imagine a world without righteousness?

The grateful leper had something the nine were missing — Faith! All ten were "cleansed" (verse 17). But only one was made "whole" (verse 19). This man's humility caused him to go find Jesus again.

> "And one of them, when he saw that he was healed, turned back, and with a loud voice glorified God, and fell down on his face at His feet, *giving Him thanks.* . ." (verses 15-16)

This man's faith led him to true gratitude. This reminds us that it is impossible to please God without faith (Hebrews 11:6). Are we behaving like the one or the nine? How often do I thank God for making me "whole"?

Thankful For Our Mission

Once I had driven through a large Texas city during rush hour and had told my wife I would never live in a place like that. Within one year God moved me to within shouting distance of that very spot! I knew it was God's will but this country boy didn't like the big city! Things went smoothly for two or three years when suddenly it seemed the city was closing in on me. I griped, I complained, I wished to be in a small place again. One day it hit me — I wasn't thankful to God for my mission anymore! My love for the country had overshadowed my love for the massive numbers of lost souls! Wonder what God thinks of an attitude like that? He sends us on the most important mission in the world and to places He especially needs us and we bellyache! There is more Jonah in us than we would like to admit!

A Crossbearer is thankful for the mission God has given him. It may be in a small spot in the road, a rugged mountain village or in a metropolis! It may be among those we "does like or doesn't like"— but we should thank God for our mission! It may be the woman in the home with her children or the teenager on the High School campus! We all have a mission and a mission point. We should praise God for that!

Explore Jesus' prayer in John 17. Shortly He will return to heaven. He is concerned about His disciples and those who would

31

come in the future. Time is growing short, the cross is in view! His prayer doesn't contain anything about food, clothes, shelter or any other physical need — His prayer zeros in on critical spiritual things. One of these concerned the mission of His disciples.

"I pray not that thou shouldest take them out of the world, but that thou shouldest keep them from the evil. They are not of this world, even as I am not of the world. Sanctify them through thy truth: thy word is truth." (verses 15-17)

Though Jesus would have liked to take His disciples to heaven with Him, He knew they had a mission to fulfill! He refused to pray that they be taken from their earthly task! Thank God they were left or we might not be Christians today! The world needed Christ's disciples; and the disciples needed the world. It was their mission field.

God still has a mission in our lives today! Our overall mission is two-fold (1) evangelizing the world (Matthew 28:19-20) and (2) equipping the saints for service (Eph. 4). Equipping the saints for what? To perform to their fullest potential in serving in the Kingdom of God! Yes, we all have been blessed with certain gifts! We all have a valuable mission on the earth! We should thank God for being a part of His great plan.

"Let the word of Christ dwell in you richly in all wisdom; teaching and admonishing one another in psalms and hymns and spiritual songs, singing with grace in your hearts to the Lord. And whatsoever you do in word or deed, do all in the name of the Lord Jesus, *giving thanks* to God and the Father by Him." (Col. 3:16-17)

A disciple is thankful for his mission!

Thankful For Our Material Blessings

At this writing there are over 12,000,000 unemployed and over 2,000,000 people homeless right here in the U.S.A. Millions are starving and homeless around the world. Last Thanksgiving day the news interviewed one unemployed man in a "tent city" outside of Houston, Texas. He said, "If you have some work, some food and a place to stay — you are a mighty blessed person." I thought how really ungrateful I had been for all my material blessings. The grateful leper in our study probably had nothing except the ragged clothes on his back and a healed body, but he was thankful! Most of us have been blessed with far more than we will ever need — are we grateful?

God was deeply upset over Israel because of their ingratitude! He still becomes upset over us today when we don't really appreciate all the things He has blessed us with. It seems the more we get, the more we desire! The more we desire the less we thank the one who is able to give.

Paul in the closing words of I Thess. shares:

> "In everything give thanks, for this is the will of God in Christ to youward." (I Thess. 5:18)

Do our prayers contain more "give me", "help me", "I need" than "I praise you", "I thank you"? If so we need to re-evaluate our prayer life and our attitude of thanksgiving! Early Christians understood these things better than we.

Conclusion

Ingratitude is a great sin of the Western world (Romans 1:21). It is heathenism! The farther we get from God — the less grateful we are! Disciples are always aware of this and this causes them to study, to pray and to work with an attitude of thanksgiving in the Lord. We are only grateful to the measure of faith we possess. It was an obedient faith that made the leper "whole" — and the same is true for us today. Our faith will lead us into a deeper appreciation of God and His blessings that have been showered upon us.

Perhaps Jesus still asks — "Where are the nine?" But praise God He still can thoroughly heal the one who says —

"I AM THANKFUL"

Questions

1. Why do you think the nine lepers failed to return and thank Jesus? Discuss.
2. Why would ingratitude be called the "respectable sin"? Discuss.
3. How would visiting a nursing home or hospital ICU waiting room help us be more thankful about being alive?
4. List and discuss five other passages of the Bible that deal with being ungrateful for our salvation.
5. What made the difference in being "cleansed" and being made "whole"?
6. Describe the main mission you are involved in at the present time.
7. What was the prayer Jesus refused to pray?
8. Should prayers be mostly thanksgiving or petition? Discuss.

Chapter Eight

"I Beseech Thee"

"Wherefore, though I might be much bold in Christ to enjoin thee that which is convenient, yet for love's sake I rather beseech thee, being such a one as Paul the aged, and now also a prisoner of Jesus Christ, I beseech thee for my son Onesimus . . . " (Philemon 8-10)

Of all the people living on the earth, Christians should be superior when it comes to human relations. Kindness, politeness, hospitality, courtesy, honesty, compassion and a tender speech are only a few of the attributes that are to be manifested in the life of a Crossbearer. This is in sharp contrast with the world's lifestyle of indulgence, selfishness, and indifference. In this chapter we want to explore how we Christians can get along with others. We might call it C. H. R. — Christian Human Relations. Our study will come from the complete letter of *Philemon*.

Here Paul found himself in an unusual situation with a good Christian friend named Philemon. Seems Philemon had a slave named Onesimus that had run away to Rome where he somehow came into contact with Paul and was converted. (verse 10) He had become a valuable co-worker. (verse 11) How Paul explains the situation and appeals to Philemon is an important lesson in human relations! It is valuable for all Christians, but especially to those in leadership capacities of the church.

Do What Is Right

We are living in a society that tends to believe there are no absolutes. We are told that everything is relative . . . situational in our behavior. This complicates good human relations instead of helping! This isn't scriptural!

Paul needed Onesimus more in Rome than Philemon needed him on the farm! Right? Sounds good, logical, doesn't it? After all, wasn't planting the gospel in a mission field more important than planting beans in Colosse? Spreading the Gospel was extremely important, but keeping Onesimus who was another man's property was *wrong!* He had broken the law; he was owned by Philemon. After considering the situation, Paul did what was RIGHT . . . not what was convenient!!

Crossbearers of Jesus Christ are to be people who are known for doing what is RIGHT! . . . No "ifs, ands, or buts"!! Children are to obey their parents in the Lord for this is convenient? No because it is RIGHT!! (Ephesians 6:1) Children of God obey their heavenly parent for the same reason.

Think how much happier we would be as individuals if we simply did what was right! Our homes would be better places in which to live. Our nation would be stronger and our churches would have more love, unity and influence. As Christians, we must do what is right in the sight of God. (Eccl. 12:13; Acts 4:19) We are not to "pervert the right ways of the Lord:" (Acts 13:10; 2 Peter 2:15) This has been God's law from the very beginning. (Gen. 4:6-7)

Paul did what he knew was right.

Am I known as one who does right . . . rather than what is convenient?

Be Nice

Not only was Paul right . . . he was also nice! 20th Century Christians urgently need to learn this lesson. We may have the truth, be absolutely right, and faithful in our convictions, but if we aren't nice we will fail to have good relations with our brothers and it is certain we will never be very evangelistic! The church will always be in turmoil. Outsiders will not be interested in our message.

Observe how Paul addresses Philemon — "Dearly beloved and fellow labourer." (verse 1) He asks about Philemon's family. (verse 2) Paul was using tact and courtesy. He calls Philemon "brother" (verses 7l, 20) and "partner" (verse 17). Disciples of Christ respect and honor one another. We address each other with this kind of attitude. Even if we are upset with another believer, we are still to address and speak to them in love! (note the introductions to all of Paul's letters)

Pray For Others

"Grace to you, and peace, from God and Our Father and the Lord Jesus Christ. I thank my God, making mention of thee always in my prayers . . ." (verses 3-4)

We should still wish "grace and peace" on all we associate within the Christian community. In our terminology today we might say, "I am praying for you . . . I'm wishing God's richest blessings upon you."

I have found in recent years that keeping a current prayer list with specific names on it can be a tremendous tool in encouraging and influencing others. When I visit these individuals, I share with them that I pray for them by name every day. Their response is always beautiful. They deeply appreciate this act of love towards them. They are encouraged, as I am, when people share this with me. Our bond as believers is strengthened and most importantly, God is acting in their lives as a result of prayer. (James 5:16)

Philemon must have also regularly prayed for Paul and the aged apostle felt if he were to ever be freed from prison, it would be the result of prayer: . . . "for I trust that through your prayers I shall be given unto you." (verse 22)

Leaders in the church should have prayer lists! In small congregations elders should pray for every member by name daily as well as other important things. In larger congregations, the membership roll may have to be divided up as in zone ministries with each elder praying for all the names on his list. The lists could be rotated among the elders periodically. Deacons could do the same. Teachers should have the names of all their students on their prayer list. Preachers should have a long prayer list including all the names possible to be adequately prayed for. Members should be encouraged to pray for one another but; until leaders in the church set this example of praying for one another . . . members certainly can't be asked to do it!!

When we do begin to pray for one another daily . . . we should share this with the ones being prayed for . . . just as Paul did to Philemon.

Compliment Others

Paul complimented Philemon concerning his love and faith for the Lord and other Christians. (verse 5) He complimented his efforts to spread the gospel. (verse 6) He mentioned Philemon's hospitality. (verse 7) As a matter of fact, in almost all of Paul's letters, we find him complimenting those he is speaking to.

How often do we tell others we appreciate them? Do we thank them for staying faithful: for the good works they are involved in? Just a little note or phone call can really boost a brother or sister onward in the cause of Christ. Call someone today and just say, "I appreciate you-you're doing a good job — hang in there"!!!

Ask, Don't Tell

"Wherefore, though I might be much bold in Christ to enjoin thee that which is convenient, yet for love's sake I rather beseech thee, being such an one as Paul the aged, and now also a prisoner of Jesus Christ. I beseech thee for my son Onesimus whom I have begotten in my bonds . . ." (verses 8-10)

Do I ask others what to do or do I order them?
Paul as an apostle of God could have "pulled rank" on Philemon; as an apostle he had the authority to order Philemon to accept Onesimus! Instead he appealed to him on the basis of love and what was right. Christians are not to "bulldog" and "arm-twist" other people! We are not to be a Diotrephes (III John 9) whose domineering tactics made him an obstacle instead of a helper! Paul would beseech (beg) Philemon. He had even asked of others "with many tears:" (2 Cor. 2:4; Acts 20:31)

Respect Others

"But without thy mind would I do nothing; that thy benefit should not be as it were of necessity, but willingly. For perhaps he therefore departed for a season, that thou shouldest receive him for ever . . ." (verses 14-15)

Paul respected Philemon. He respected him so much that he wasn't willing to chance damaging his relationship with this good brother at Colosse. Without Philemon's consent he did not want to do anything except what he knew was best. He hoped Philemon would react spontaneously instead of out of necessity. This is an excellent example of putting others before self which Paul had often preached. Here we see him practicing what he preached.

> "Give none offense, neither to the Jews, nor to the Gentiles, nor to the church of God; Even as I please all men in all things, not seeking mine own profit, but the profit of many that they may be saved. Be followers of me, even as I also am of Christ." (1 Corinthians 10:32–11:1)

This passage challenges us as disciples of Christ to take on this same image.

Share Your Trust

> "Yea, brother, let me have joy of thee in the word; refresh my bowels (heart) in the Lord. Having confidence in thy obedience I wrote unto thee, knowing that thou wilt also do more than I say." (verses 20–21)

Paul was telling his friend, "I believe in you . . . I trust you . . . I have confidence in you . . . You will do even more than I request! . . . You will go the second mile." People must not only be loved and praised . . . they also must experience your trust! Think! . . . how long has it been since you communicated to a fellow believer your confidence, your trust in them? It isn't enough just to think it . . . we must say it and say it often. This is true with all the attitudes we have explored in this book. They will never know how much we care until we open our mouths and tell them!

Lead, Don't Shove

I am confident Philemon received Onesimus as a brother in Christ (verse 16) mainly because of Paul's loving, influential letter and the relationship they had built up between themselves over the years. What if Paul though had written in a harsh, demanding manner? Like us, Philemon would not have appreciated that kind of attitude from a fellow Christian . . . even if he were an apostle! Too many in God's kingdom still haven't learned this lesson. Some leaders harshly "lord over" their sheep, speaking to them in abrasive and demanding ways never intended by the Lord. Some preachers likewise "brow beat" members-using the pulpit to get a few straightened out! Meanwhile, sheep who have no choice about being there (like Onesimus) are frightened, discouraged, even lost. We can become stumbling blocks right in the church house! Jesus didn't come to *drive* sheep anywhere! He came to *lead* and perhaps more importantly to *draw* them unto him. (John 12:32) Shepherds today must understand the attributes of a Shepherd found in John 10 before they will ever understand those in Timothy and Titus! Paul knew his sheep. He could call them by name. He was a gentle shepherd.

Results

The next Sunday when Philemon and Onesimus worshipped as "brothers in Christ" . . . don't you know Onesimus thanked the Lord that Paul and Philemon had the kind of relationship they did? Under Roman Law he could have been killed! Christianity made the difference! Being "in Christ" empowered Philemon to be forgiving and gave Onesimus the hope that he would. Onesimus still needed an advocate, Paul. This reminds us that Christ is our advocate. We too deserved death but Christ took our place. He is to be the Lord of our life. As a Crossbearer we are becoming more and more like Him. We are able to rid ourselves of ungodly attitudes and fill the void with righteousness. Like Onesimus, we "departed for a season" but now are "servants and brothers" to each other and to the Lord. With this in mind, we are able to humbly "beseech" others instead of demanding. Our relationship with the Lord compels us to be right and to be nice.

Questions

1. Discuss why Christians are to do what is right rather than what is convenient.
2. In our communication with one another, why is it so important we be nice, even if we are upset with that person?
3. How does having the *truth* without being *nice* remind you of 1 Corinthians 13?
4. Discuss the fruits of maintaining a current prayer list.
5. Discuss using tact with others in relation to Jesus' words in Matthew 7:12.
6. Why is it important to verbally express our feelings of trust, respect and appreciation to others?

Chapter Nine

"I Am A Sinner"

"And I thank Christ Jesus our Lord, who hath enabled me, for that he counted me faithful, putting me into the ministry; who was before a blasphemer, and a persecutor, and injurious: but I obtained mercy, because I did it ignorantly in unbelief. And the grace of our Lord was exceeding abundant with faith and love which is in Christ Jesus. This is a faithful saying, and worthy of all acceptation, that Christ Jesus came into the world to save sinners; of whom I am chief. Howbeit for this cause I obtained mercy, that in me, first Jesus Christ might shew forth all longsuffering, for a pattern to them which should hereafter believe on him to life everlasting. Now unto the King eternal, immortal, invisible, the only wise God, be honour and glory for ever and ever. Amen."

1 Timothy 1:12–17

Introduction

Disciples (Cross-Bearers) live by faith; their faith involves many foundational statements or principles which may or may not be verbalized. The issue of life is sin . . . disciples not only understand sin they commit themselves to their saviour. Many comprehend alien (past) sins but not present sins as saints. The idea of eternal security (once saved, always saved) is wrong; however eternal insecurity is equally wrong. The 3 G's (guilt, grace, gratitude) belong to Christians. They understand sin, salvation , and sanctification. Someone has observed there are only two kind of sinners — lost sinners and forgiven sinners. Christians sin, but Christians also live in grace. Christians are sinners; they also are forgiven sinners. Christians are not sinlessly perfect; their faith is in Christ their saviour.

I Was A Sinner

Paul remonstrates about his alien sins! He named blasphemy, persecution, yea murder! Paul was a "chief sinner" as a sinner. He confessed his sins. To sin is man's condition; to pretend that he is not a sinner is man's greatest sin. Heaven will be occupied by those who know they sin; hell will be occupied by those who think they are good without sin. They would need a sense of sin (John 16:7–10).

Paul said this to emphasize the riches of the grace of God. Jesus came to save sinners (Luke 19:10); Jesus calls sinners, not the righteous (Mt. 9:12, 13). Paul accepted the grace of God. (1 Cor. 15:10) Paul gives hope to all sinners. If the grace of God could save him, it could save all. Paul says, "Look at me; I am Exhibit A!" "Is there any hope for me?" *YES-YES-YES!*

Paul did not live in morbid guilt. He did not travel all over the world promoting himself as evil glorying in his sin. Paul did not have a neurotic guilt. It takes self-affirmation to practice self-denial. Paul did not have an inverted pride which says, "He can save other people but not me". Paul never considered himself as one "who had committed the unpardonable sin". Paul knew sin but even more he accepted grace! How dare one think there is grace for others but not him!

This is a vital lesson. David in the Old Testament sinned grievously. He confessed his sins simply and without explanation. However, the greatness of David was not contained in such confession! The glory of David was that he equally accepted God's forgiveness. No man has the right to remember what God has forgiven/forgotten. Some are harder on themselves than God! Someone said Peter could never hear a rooster crow without crying. True! But not from guilt still prized but forgiveness accepted! Jesus did not come to awaken guilt to condemn but to save.

I Am Saved By Grace

Paul was saved by grace not merit. His focus was upon Christ not his merited works. Paul did not recommend himself to others; he did recommend Jesus Christ to all. If we think we know how to run our own lives Jesus can never be accepted as King of our lives. From our text Paul attributes his salvation to mercy and grace. Paul was a preacher and practitioner of grace. He began and ended his epistles with "grace and peace". Said salutations were not to be considered merely as salutations. Paul sums up the cause and effect — grace and peace. This is what Christianity is.

Too many preach grace while living (practicing) on merit. The human tendency is "will power" not "faith (Christ) power". Salvation by works presumes to do what God only can do (Psa. 19:13; Rom. 3:22-27; 4:16; 11:6, 33-36). Paul's faith was in Christ, not Paul. His obedience was not to earn this love but out of this love! This distinction is crucial. The only permanent motivation in Christianity is grace. There is another observation that is crucial — Paul was "sick of sin" not "sick of self". Paul openly confessed sin yet did not "run himself down". Jesus came and dealt with the sin problem. Paul knew that even the greatest saint sins, needs God, is saved only by grace.

Noah got drunk, Moses lost his temper, Gideon was scared, Peter sank in the Sea of Galilee, Thomas doubted, and even Martha pouted! Christianity is a very humbling religion. From Jesus we learn that we can never save ourselves. By the grace of God in Christ I can now be saved! There is no glorying on my part, Jesus paid it all! *GET THIS!* "Jesus paid it all". My faith is in Christ at His cross. Repentance comes from this goodness of God! My confession of faith is Christ my Lord. I am baptized into Him claiming all His promises. Being born again my life is His life. All my claims

42

focus upon Jesus! This is the tragedy of Phariseeism — there is no room for Jesus!

The only good in Paul (all Christians) was the Christ in Paul! God said on two occasions, "This is my Beloved Son in whom I am well pleased". God is pleased with Christians because of Christ. Man's sin problem is turned over to God! There could be no greater sin than to take advantage of the grace of God! Grace is no "blue-eyed blond". Grace demands. "What shall we say then? Shall we continue in sin, live any longer therein?" (Rom. 6:1, 2) Paul kept the grace of God pure and holy. Paul never considered himself too unworthy to accept the unearned, unmerited, undeserved grace of God.

Peter learned this the hard way. In Acts 10 God came to Peter in a vision. All manner of animals, clean and unclean, were presented to be eaten. Peter said, "Not so, Lord" (Acts 10:14). Now this statement is a contradiction. As one said it is "one or the tuther". If it is "not so" then Jesus is not Lord. If Jesus is Lord then one cannot rebel saying, "not so". Paul made Jesus the King (ruler) of his heart. Paul did not have faith in his obedience — his obedience came from faith (Rom. 1:5; 16:26). Paul's faith gloried in God's grace. Peter learned in Acts 10 the Lordship of Christ. Will power can never purify the heart; obedience to God's grace can.

This, to a degree, explains 2 Corinthians 12. In 2 Corinthians 11 Paul felt coerced to defend his apostleship with his dedication. This embarrassed Paul yet his actions were necessary, "Are they ministers of Christ? (I speak as a fool) I am more; in labours more abundant, in stripes above measure, in prisons more frequent, in deaths oft". (2 Cor. 11:23). All preachers (including most Christians) idolize Paul. Seemingly he is the epitome of works! He makes one ashamed of his dedication. All wish to work like Paul. Then, wham, we have 2 Corinthians 12! Paul, a man who suffered more, is allowed a thorn! Seemingly he had enough trouble! Why burden your giant with a thorn? The answer is grace! The thorn kept Paul's faith on God and off Paul!" "And lest I should be exalted above measure through the abundance of the revelations, there was given to me a thorn in the flesh, the messenger of Satan to buffet me, lest I should be exalted above measure . . . and he said unto me, my grace is sufficient for thee: for my strength is made perfect in weakness" (2 Cor. 12:7-9).

I Am The Chiefest Sinner

Tragically many have failed to notice the tense in Paul's statement. He changes from who he was to who he is. Paul did not say, "I was the chiefest". He said, "I am the chiefest". All disciples (Cross-bearers) make this statement. We not only confess our past needs but our present needs. We not only confess a Savior past but a Savior present! Most do not know how to handle daily Christian living. What happens to Christians in daily living involving human weakness, ignorance, and sin? Must all Christians be restored every Sunday? Did God save us by grace only to return us back to human effort? Did God, to Christians, drop the Bible out of the sky saying, "Good Luck?" Is Christianity, in reality, only humanism? Is man to do the best he can under his own resource? Does one preach guilt to Christians or grace? Do Christians walk a tightrope while living and die with their fingers crossed? Is this faith or fear? Can Christians sleep at night having failed during the day?

What does Paul teach by being an "I am" sinner! He confesses daily needs, daily sins. He confesses a present condition. Christians need grace for past sins; they equally need grace for daily sins. Our faith lies in grace. Grace, to Paul, was not only God's purging power for the past but His enabling strength in the present. Christians live in daily sin; they also live in daily grace! "I live in sin yet I live in grace."

Paul confessed his sinfulness. David was not a man after God's own heart because he did not sin! David was an adulterer, murderer, and cheat! However, David confessed his sin and accepted God's grace. Paul knew it required grace to be saved; it equally requires grace to remain saved. Paul knew the worst about himself. He knew he was capable of blasphemy and violence. He knew without God he was defeated. Daily sin demands daily grace. The main idea in our text is not past alien sin but present, daily needs. Security is in grace not performance. There is always that something I needed to know or do! Christians are saved at the cross; they are equally kept at the cross.

Paul, in our text, commands Christians to *continue* as they *began.* "As ye have therefore received Christ Jesus the Lord, so walk ye in him" (Col. 2:6). Christ is our life (Col. 3:1-4). "Are ye so foolish, having begun in the Spirit, are ye now made perfect by the flesh? (Gal. 3:3) Christians are accepted "in the Beloved" (Eph. 1:6). Too many have the false idea that "only good people can go to church". But the church is not a "Hotel for Saints"; it is a "Hospital for Sinners". God is running an "Emergency Room". Christians cannot be intimidated by sin! The glory of grace is that God uses imperfect, immoral, dishonest people! All the holy men have gone off and died! No one is left but "us sinners". Accept the grace of God!

Questions
1. What do we really mean when we say, "I am a sinner"?
2. Discuss the error both in "Eternal Security" and "Eternal Insecurity".
3. Why did Paul refer to his past, forgiven sins? Did he live in neurotic guilt? What was Paul's favorite word?

4. Discuss David in detail.
5. Do we preach grace while practicing merit?
6. What sin could be greater than taking advantage of the grace of God?
7. Discuss Peter in Acts 10:14.
8. Why the thorn given Paul in 2 Corinthians 12?
9. Is the statement of Paul "I was" or "I am" the worst of sinners? Does one need daily grace? Do we live in sin and in grace? Discuss "to continue as we began".

Chapter Ten

"I Am Crucified With Christ"

"I am crucified with Christ: nevertheless I live; yet not I, but Christ liveth in me: and the life which I now live in the flesh I live by the faith of the Son of God, who loved me, and gave himself for me. I do not frustrate the grace of God: for if righteousness come by the law, then Christ is dead in vain".

Gal. 2:20, 21

Introduction

REMEMBER!! Familiar scriptures have to be read more closely. The second time you read a scripture you usually read your concept rather than the words. This is a great statement of Paul. It deserves our total acceptance. It is not merely to be stated but lived. Let us take the statement and break it down into practical observation.

"I Am"

Many suffer from poor self-esteem. Our favorite phrase in a song says, "for such a worm as I". We like to think of ourselves as "worms". We are sinners, but not worms! Man is not less than animals. God does not love worms (John 3:16); Jesus did not die for worms. It is a sin to "run others down"; it is equally a sin to "run yourself down". Too low self-esteem says, "I don't think I can". But, "I don't think I can" rises from the deeper, "I don't think I am". God's grace is no problem to me regarding others. It is easy to convince sinners of John 3:16; Rom. 5:6–8; 1 John 4:7–11. Then what is the problem? The problem is accepting God's grace to *ME!* In a recent evaluation one religious group was characterized two ways: (1) They had poor self-esteem, and (2) They could not get along with anyone. It is hard for me to accept God's grace! Why? Because such grace gives me worth, dignity, acceptance. I do not wish to forgive myself! I do not wish to give up my inferiority! I do not wish to give up my "crutch"! But "I am", therefore "I can". One saved cannot be considered worthless. The "I am" will always determine the "I can". Because "I am" somebody "I can" do things.

Too much in religion has promoted insecurity. We have preached guilt but not grace. Sensitive hearts have been manipulated, promoted, and exploited. This explains why some religionists are hostile, frustrated, and even neurotic. We cannot accept as a viable, valued faith any religion that fails to produce emotionally healthier human beings. "For God hath not given us the spirit of fear; but of power, and of love, and of a sound mind" (2 Tim. 1:7). Jesus does not make men mad, mean, nor ill! Jesus makes men whole.

So what is our beef? We feel too unworthy to accept unearned unmerited, undeserved forgiveness! We do not consider ourselves worthy of the cross. We tend to think we have sinned "too big" or "gone too far" to be saved. We simply do not value ourselves enough to believe that we can truly be loved unconditionally and nonjudgmentally. So we resist salvation by grace! We fight it . . . run from it . . . deny it! Our shame of unworthiness compels us to believe we must do something to "earn love" or "merit salvation". So we perform to be accepted rather than be accepted to perform. We try to work our way up to grace rather than allow grace to work in us. We believe in achieving rather than believing. We believe in ourselves rather than in God.

Someone said, "I am not what I think I am. I am not what you think I am. I am what I think you think I am". This may be true with people but not with Paul. Paul was what God thought he was! Paul found his worth, esteem in Christ! Grace claimed Paul! The crucifixion of Christ placed God's value upon Paul. "Who was before a blasphemer, and a persecutor, and injurious: but I obtained mercy, because I did it ignorantly in unbelief, and the grace of our Lord was exceeding abundant with faith and love which is in Christ Jesus. This is a faithful saying, and worthy of all acceptation, that Christ Jesus came into the world to save sinners; of whom I am chief. Howbeit for this cause I obtained mercy, that in me first Jesus Christ might shew forth all longsuffering, for a pattern to them which should hereafter believe on him to life everlasting" (1 Tim. 1:13-16). Everything Paul was came by the grace of God (1 Cor. 15:10; 2 Cor. 12:9).

This is the Gospel (Good News). Christ is our hope of glory (Col. 1:27, 28). In His incarnation Christ honored the human race by joining it. At the cross Christ placed an unlimited value upon the human soul. With the resurrection Jesus allows us into His ministry with power (Phil. 3:9, 10). This is why sinners want the Gospel and religionists fight it! The Gospel is positive, not negative; polite, not rude; kind, not mean; constructive, not destructive, and beautiful, not ugly!

I Am Crucified

Christianity is one thing — a cross. The Christian life is a crucified life. This is not poetry but practical living. ". . . If any man will come after me, let him deny himself, and take up his cross, and follow me. For whosoever will save his life shall lose it: and whosoever will lose his life for my sake shall find it." (Mt. 16:24, 25). "If any man come to me, and hate not his father, and mother and wife, and children, and brethren, and sisters, yea, and his own life also, he cannot be my disciple. And whosoever doth not bear his cross, and come after me, cannot be my disciple"

(Luke 14:26, 27). Paul simply said, "I die daily" (1 Cor. 15:31). Simply stated, we die to live.

That's the rub! Men resist death. We want a Christianity without a cross, a life without a cost. But life teaches we die to live. Seed dies to live; men die for causes; in the resurrection something must go in before something can come out. Sinners die to self and to sin (Rom. 6:1-18). The fundamental in life is dying to live, dying to reproduce. Jesus calls us to die. One cannot hurt a dead man; one cannot kill a dead man. The man who has given up everything can give up anything. We cannot have peace without purity, forgiveness without change, strength without discipline. We cannot be cured without being conquered. Jesus must become the Lord of our life. The problem is not world evangelism — the problem is "church-crucifixion".

> A church that will not bleed cannot bless.
> A church that will not suffer cannot save.
> A church that will not die cannot live.

Alabaster boxes have to be broken; God uses only broken things. "Verily, verily, I say unto you, except a corn of wheat fall into the ground and die, it abideth alone: but if it die, it bringeth forth much fruit." (John 12:24). "And I, if I be lifted up from the earth, will draw all men unto me. This he said, signifying what death he should die. (John 12:32, 33)

I Am Crucified With Christ
"But God forbid that I should glory, save in the cross of our Lord Jesus Christ, by whom the world is crucified unto me, and I unto the world. For in Christ Jesus neither circumcision availeth anything, nor uncircumcision, but a new creature (Gal. 6:14, 15). In Romans Christ died for us; in Romans 6 we died with him. This is life participation. The crux of Romans 6 is not baptism (3 times) but death (16 times). In baptism we die with Jesus. Peter tried to talk Jesus out of dying (Mt. 16). Jesus told Peter this is exactly what *BOTH* had to do.

Nevertheless I Live
This is the glory of our text. Although crucified (dead) Paul lived. Read our text and count the repeated times Paul said, "I live". Now turn in Ephesians 3:14-19. This is one of the great Bible segments. Now use your imagination. Play like you have a stalk of corn. A beautiful, green, healthy stalk of corn! Now command the cornstalk to make corn. Right now, manufacture corn! Can a cornstalk make corn? Paradoxically, it cannot. Corn is fruit; fruit cannot be manufactured. Only God can make corn. God bears corn on

a cornstalk. Only God can make Christians. Jesus is the only man who can live the Christian life. Jesus can live the Christian life in me; God can bear fruit in me (John 15).

One should not try to live the Christian life; he should live life as a Christian. This distinction is vital. Back to our imaginary cornstalk. A cornstalk cannot put out what it has not brought in! A cornstalk is at the mercy of its intake. Put a cornstalk in poor soil without water, sun, or minerals and it cannot produce. Put it in and the cornstalk will produce. Any farmer knows this! You do not get offended at cornstalks during a drouth! You cannot expect of a cornstalk without intake!

The same is true of Christians. Christians cannot put out what they have not brought in. Christianity is no self-improvement course. In fact, there is no self-improvement course that improves people very much. Christianity is Christ. Christianity is not, "go-go-go" and "more-more-more". It is *CHRIST-CHRIST-CHRIST!* From Ephesians 3:14–19 Paul reveals the four things Christians need:

INNER STRENGTH Temples are indwelled by God. Christians are temples (1 Cor. 3:16, 17; 6:19, 20). The Holy Spirit is the Christians' Partner (Acts 2:38). All the promises of Jesus (John 14–17) were connected in the "paraclete", the Holy Spirit. Christianity is "an inside job". We are a new creation (John 3:3, 5, 7; 2 Cor. 5:17; Gal. 6:14, 15). We are partakers of the divine nature (2 Pet. 1:4).

IN CHRIST Sinners must "put on Christ" (Gal. 3:26, 27). Paul used the phrase, "in Christ" 164 times. I may not can love an enemy — but Christ can! I may not be able but Christ is (Phil. 4:13). His righteousness is mine (Phil. 3:9, 10). Christ is "my life" (Col. 3:1–4).

GROUNDED IN LOVE This is an arresting thought and contradicts the world's maudlin sentimentality given love. Paul says love is stable. The four substantives used describe the fullness of the love of God. Paul says this love exceeds our abilities. Christ's love motivates us (2 Cor. 5:14). The greater capacity one has to grasp this love the more spiritual power one has.

THE FULLNESS OF GOD This is mind-boggling! If God could be bottled how much would one ounce cost? Is God stingy? *NO!* God is willing to give us *ALL* we will receive. We bring in to put out. We cannot put out what we have not brought in. Christians are filled with God.

Questions

1. Discuss a point made repeatedly, "Familiar scriptures must be read more closely".
2. Are we "worms"? Discuss this. Does grace give proper self-esteem? Discuss "I Am" therefore "I Can".

3. Are we unworthy of the cross? Could one unworthy's love be worth anything?
4. Discuss Paul in 1 Timothy 1:12-16.
5. Discuss the crucified life.
6. Discuss our wanting Christianity without a cross. Discuss alabaster boxes.
7. Illustrate with the "cornstalk" as you would.
8. Study in depth Ephesians 3:14-19.

Chapter Eleven

I Press On

A Dallas bank has a unique TV commercial explaining the reason for their great success. They say the secret is "momentum" — always moving forward! Everyone is urged to use their bank because they have got what it takes to reach the top even in these hard economic days.

Nothing ever goes forward without momentum! Spiritual momentum is a quality Christ's disciples must possess as they march forward in the cause of the Master. God has a myriad of faithful, motivated Christians in His Kingdom today. Praise God for that! But there are also just as many souls across this land who are prodigals. Somewhere along the way they either "burned out, dropped out or were snuffed out." There are also many weak, milk-of-the-word Christians in our Churches. What keeps a disciple motivated, moving forward, and experiencing dynamic, life-changing, fruitbearing faith? From where does spiritual momentum come?

The apostle Paul serves as an example of one who ignited at conversion and blazed a shining path through a dark, crooked, and perverse world (Phil. 2:15–16). When Paul's life ended, his light did not go out — he left this world a ball of fire! We are still illuminated by his life today. The secret to the apostle's momentum is found in Philippians 3:13–14.

> "Brethren, I count not myself to have apprehended: but this one thing I do, forgetting those things which are behind, and reaching forth unto those things which are before. I press toward the mark for the prize of the high calling of God in Christ Jesus."

Paul was a disciple, a cross-bearer of Jesus Christ. He was "in Christ" — which began in his conversion (Acts 22). He had received "a high calling" (Phil. 3:14) which transformed a murdering, Roman soldier into a devout servant of God! Paul's relationship to the Lord grew stronger and stronger as his life went by. The road to victory was "a straight and narrow way." Though the road was a tough struggle, each step and each day brought him ever closer to his mark (goal).

Like Paul, we Christians today find ourselves in this same struggle. It's easy to become a Christian, but hard to remain a disciple! In Philippians 3 Paul is teaching us that reaching "the mark" is accomplished two important ways. *First,* we must be "forgetting the things which are behind." *Secondly,* we are to be "reaching forth unto those things which are before." Notice that both of these phrases are in the present tense; both are a continuing process.

When we Christians practice this formula, we will develop the "one mind" (Phil. 1:27). ". . . this one thing I do" (Phil. 3:13) . . . "I press on" (Phil. 3:14, NKJV).

Basically, human nature hasn't changed since these words were penned by inspiration of the Holy Spirit. We still have trouble "hanging in there." Seminars, lectureship, talk shows, books and tapes abound today on the subject of motivation, momentum — success. Much of this self-help pop psychology has been a failure. Why do Christian people turn to the "world" for answers in spiritual matters? Let us return to the Book that gives God's answers!

Paul is a wonderful example of a cross-bearer who was motivated, dynamic, solid as a rock! He was faithful unto death! (2 Tim. 4:6-8; Rev. 2:10) He had momentum. He could joyfully write from a prison cell — "I press on!" Let us examine Paul's spiritual momentum a little more closely and see how this can help us be better disciples today.

"Forgetting the past" — disciples of Christ walk in the light of today and the hope of tomorrow, not in the shadows of the past! It isn't wrong to recall and learn from the past. (Heb. 10:32; Rom. 15:9) But, when we allow our minds to continually focus on the past, it can become a hindrance to our faith. Many Bible examples warn us about looking backward. (Gen. 19:26; Ex. 14:10-13; Lk. 9:62; John 21:20; Heb. 12:1-3) No one can maintain forward momentum while looking backward! Paul knew if he spent all his time thinking and worrying about the past, he could become a dropout in the Christian race — he could lose his momentum.

We have all seen football players break for the goal line leaving all the opposing team members behind — only to be caught. At some point they looked back losing their stride — their momentum. The same thing happens in the lives of Christians today! (Gal. 3:1ff) Dwelling on our past defeats — even on our victories — can distract us.

Suppose Paul had begun feeling sorry for himself in that Roman prison and had let his mind wander back to some of his many defeats. Wasted years before conversion, regular illness, imprisonment, beatings, shipwrecks, loneliness, fear, Church factions, unfaithful Christians, deserted partners, loss of friends and home, financial loss, past sins, unused opportunities, unevangelized cities and countries, immorality among believers, mistakes, unbelieving friends and family — and many more. Do any of these ring a bell with us? Which ones capture our thinking? Some Christians today have trouble forgetting their past defeats. "If I had had a better childhood," "If my parents," "If the Church I attended," "I was just too young," "Only a third grade education," "The war," "I was raised in the Depression," and on and on! God isn't interested in our past defeats! We must not let the past hinder us from pressing on!

Suppose Paul had become obsessed with all his past victories — called to be an apostle, a Roman officer, a Pharisee, a great lineage, well-educated, student of Gamaliel, speaker to kings and queens, healings, spiritual growth — he could have let his past victories conquer him. How many disciples today have become entangled in "the good ol' days" illusion? "I had twenty converts last year," "I was baptized by George Super Preacher," "I wish we had revivals like when I was young." Jesus warns "remember Lot's wife" (Lk. 17:32).

Forgetting the past also includes "laying aside every weight and sin which doth so easily beset us . . ." (Heb. 12:1). Christians must learn how to leave their past sins and the guilt of those sins at the cross! When God forgives, He forgets! When we pray do we continue to ask God to forgive sins we have already confessed? How often must we ask His forgiveness of a sin? Do we really believe He forgives? Let's not become bogged down over the sins of which we have already been forgiven.

> "If we walk in the light, as he is in the light, we have fellowship one with another, and the blood of Jesus Christ his Son cleanseth us from *all sin*" . . . "if we confess our sins, he is faithful and just to forgive us our sins, and to cleanse us from all unrighteousness." (1 John 1:7, 9)

Paul had past defeats, victories, yes — sins, but look what he did with them? (Phil. 3:7-8) They were counted as loss. They were put behind him!

"Reaching forth unto those things which are before" — Paul's body was in a cold prison cell, but his mind was in heaven! He was free! Disciples are to be spiritually minded (Rom. 8:5ff; Phil. 1:27). We are to keep our minds in heaven (Phil. 3:20) and on heavenly things (Phil. 4:8-9; Col. 2:3; 3:1). Jesus taught the same thing (Matt. 6:21; 13:44; Mk. 10:21).

Christians must keep their eyes on the goal (mark)! We are to be distance runners! We are in the marathon of life. We are not running to be saved, but because we are saved! Paul was already in the race — a "perfect" (mature) disciple (Phil. 3:13) but he was pressing on toward the goal of glorious, resurrected perfection (Phil. 3:10, 20). This he would experience at the second coming of the Lord. (Phil. 3:10-11; 20-21; 1 Thess. 2:19).

Like Paul we are following Jesus "the forerunner" (Heb. 6:20) and Jesus "the pioneer" (Greek *archegos*) and perfector of our faith." (Heb. 12:2) Jesus has traveled the way we are going! He faced the same temptations (Heb. 4:14-16) as we do and He overcame. He arose victorious from the grave. We follow in His steps!

Paul challenges us, "Be ye followers of me as I am of Christ" (1 Cor. 11:1; 9:24).

So, spiritual momentum is maintained by forgetting the past and pressing on to the future. The key to keeping this attitude is love. Paul was motivated, propelled by God's love for Him. "I live by the faith of the Son of God, who *loved me,* and gave himself for me." (Gal. 2:20b) We are *not* primarily motivated by our love for God and what we can do for Him; we are motivated by God's love for us and what He has done for us. "We love him because he first loved us." (1 John 4:19; 1 John 3:1; 3:16; Gal. 1:15; Eph. 1:7; 2:4-10, 13; Titus 3:5) Our response to God's love for us is the propellant that keeps us "Pressing on." With it we can continue forgetting the past and keep reaching toward the mark. Our brotherly love for others comes only when we allow God's love to fill us. We become fruitful; we attract others when we exhibit love (Jno. 13:35).

Paul was not alone as he ran toward the mark; neither are we. When God calls us (2 Thess. 2:14), and apprehends us (Phil. 3:12), and "adds us to the church" (Acts 2:47), He also empowers us to accomplish the assigned task — to reach our goal! Disciples who are "in Christ" are assured God will see us through!

"I can do all things through Christ which strengtheneth me" (Phil. 4:13). He will never leave us or forsake us (Heb. 13:5-6). God goes with us in all that we do. (Eph. 3:20; Col. 1:11; 2 Tim. 1:14; 4:17; Heb. 13:6) The Holy Spirit comforts us; He is our helper. (John 14:16-17, 26; 15:26; 16:7-14; Rom. 8:1-27; 14:17; 1 Cor. 3:16; 6:11; 2 Cor. 1:22; 3:3, 8-18; Gal. 5:5, 17-25; 2 Tim. 1:7, 14; 1 John 2:20; 3:24; 4:2, 13)

Of course, Christians can never experience any of God's love and power unless their minds are absorbed in the word (Rom. 1:16-17) and in prayer (Phil. 4:6). Great marathons are run one step at a time with our eyes fixed on the goal. Our mind must see further than our eyes! Running the marathon of life requires living one day at a time for God. It's a daily process. *"Today,* if you hear his voice," (Heb. 3:7). *"Daily"* (Acts). "But encourage one another *daily* as long as it is called *today* so that none of you may be hardened by sin's deceitfulness." (Heb. 3:13). The book of Hebrews is saying, "I know you are having a struggle, but hang in there!" A key word found throughout this encouraging letter is *TODAY.*

Paul could clearly see the end! He had been following the steps of one who brought him ever close to the goal. He was running to the *Son*rise, not the sunset! He had hope in judgment (1 Thess. 1:3, 10; 2 Cor. 3:12ff; Heb. 7:25). He was aware of Paradise and its glories (2 Cor. 12:1-6) and he wasn't about to miss the real thing! We Christians today also run this same race with hope, confidence and power! (1 John 5:13) As we run, let us encourage others along the way! Search all the "one another" verses in the New Testament. As we run, we light the way for others who follow us, as we follow Jesus and Paul.

> "For I am now ready to be offered, and the time of my departure is at hand. I have fought a good fight, I have finished my course, I have kept the faith! Henceforth there is laid up for me a crown of righteousness, which the Lord, the righteous judge, shall give me at that day: and not to me only, but unto all them that love his appearing."
>
> (2 Tim. 4:6-8)

The cross bearer says, "I PRESS ON."

Questions

1. Discuss why it is so important that we leave our sins at the cross.
2. Both "forgetting the past" and "reaching forth" are in the present tense. What is the significance of this?
3. "Our response to God's love is the propellant that keeps us pressing on." Discuss.
4. God gives us an excellent lesson in Philippians 3 on setting and reaching goals. What are your goals in the following time frames:

    Immediate—

    Five Year—

    Ten Year—

    Long Range—

5. How can dwelling on the past distract us in running the Christian race?

May 22

Chapter Twelve

I Believe In You

"Having confidence in thy obedience I wrote unto thee, knowing that thou wilt also do more than I say."

Philemon 21

"For I know the forwardness of your mind, for which I boast of you to them of Macedonia, that Achaia was ready a year ago; and your zeal hath provoked very many.

Yet have I sent the brethren, lest our boasting of you should be in vain in this behalf; that, as I said, ye may be ready:

Lest haply if they of Macedonia come with me, and find you unprepared, we (that we say not, ye) should be ashamed in the same confident boasting."

2 Corinthians 9:2-4

Introduction

TRUST! The needed ingredient in faith today. Not merely mental assent, not merely dutiful obedience — but *TRUST!* Disciples trust; disciples are trustworthy; disciples are trusted. The word pistos has both an active and passive sense, that is, trusting and trustworthy. In the Old Testament the passive prevails (fidelity), and in the New Testament the active prevails (trusting). What the world needs most of all is trust.

But the fact denies the need. The world is suspicious; this even touches brethren. Elders must trust preachers, preachers must trust deacons, deacons must trust members, members must trust elders! Great churches can only be built upon mutual trust. Congregations must trust each other. Issues, factions, nit-picking must cease.

At a seminar men were introducing themselves and naming their job. To break the monotony one man said, "My job is to make my boss look good." How poignant! If only husbands/wives lived to make mates look good! It is not my love for my wife that keeps me faithful — it is the knowledge she loves me! Read 2 Cor. 5:14 — it is not my love for Christ but His love for me that motivates. To trust, to be trusted are sacred privileges. Disciples believe in others! Barnabas believed in John Mark and Saul! Jesus believed in Peter and Matthew! Paul believed in Philemon. People must be believed in — they will live up to our expectations. Someone observed, "I am not what I think I am; I am not what you think I am; I am what I think you think I am". Trusted people change and work! Christian lives are built upon trust. Life is worth living; people are worth loving; God is worth trusting.

I Believe In God

Read Psalm 100! "Know ye that the Lord he is God: it is he that hath made us, and not we ourselves; we are his people, and the sheep of his pasture" (verse 3). God is! Disciples believe that God is.

But this is not sufficient. This explains why evidences although valid are limited. One must also know that God is good! "For the Lord is good; his mercy is everlasting; and his truth endureth to all generations. We must do more than convince our children that God is! Atheism, by the way, is not in the head — it is in the heart (Psalms 14:1). We must secure our children believing that God is good! This begins with praise, when times are hard praise God! Too many expect little of God and are not disappointed. Others cry, "I tried prayer and it did not work". One cannot worship a disappointment! A disciple trusts God; he believes God knows what he is doing. A disciple knows God is more ready to guide us than we are willing to be guided! Christianity is still a "God" religion! Jesus came to reveal God! Job said, "Though he slay me, yet will I trust in him" (Job 13:15). Disciples not only believe in eternal life; they live abundant life. Faith is mental assent, whole-hearted trust, and total obedience (Heb. 11:6).

There is more! God trusts me! Many are afraid to turn their lives over to God because they are not sure they will be satisfied with what God had in mind. A faith that cannot be tested cannot be trusted! Disciples believe in God; God believes in disciples. Read 1 Peter 1:1-10, God trusts us more than we trust ourselves. All easily accept heaven — God is preparing a place for us. Few accept the other side — God is preparing us for that place! Why would God make heaven if no one came! My parents had me, their only child, late in life. They worked to have a farm for me. Without me that farm is without meaning! Heaven, without us, is without meaning! God trusted the Gospel to us! In a poem "The Advent" by Betty W. Talbert, there is this conclusion:

No rational God would trust me with a baby.
No rational God would trust me.
No rational God would trust.
The burden of Nativity that penetrates to bother me
Is not that I trust God
But that He trusts me
WITH HIMSELF.

I Believe In Myself

The problem in life and the challenge in Christianity is to simply, "Be Myself." What does one do with himself? He is stuck with himself both now and throughout eternity. In a recent Tennessee research involving seven religions this is the evaluation of one — "Having poor self-esteem they cannot get along with anyone". What one thinks of himself is vital for worthwhile living. How one sees oneself determines how one lives. Everyone has a relationship with himself either good or bad.

Does the Bible teach "self love" or "self hate"? Read Mt. 22:35-40, ". . . Thou shalt love thy neighbor as thyself". Our problems with others comes with a fault within ourselves. Read Eph. 5:22-23, ". . . so ought men to love their wives as their own bodies. He that loveth his wife loveth himself. For no man ever yet hated his own flesh; but nourisheth and cherisheth it, even as the Lord the church."

Vanity, pride, inflated egotism are wrong! But pride in the form of humility is equally wrong. Inverted pride is also wrong. To run yourself down is as wrong as running others down. Guilt must not be preached without grace. The mentality that preaching makes one feel worse must be avoided! "I don't feel good unless the preacher makes me feel bad!" Even many of the "Wednesday Night Bunch" (the best) seriously think they have committed the "unpardonable sin". Christians must not focus upon their sins but their Savior! Self Love is not preoccupation with self. "Get your mind off yourself and yourself off your mind." Self love is neither to be inferior nor superior. Self love is simply to be one's self. All need a self he can live with.

Christianity is not an inferiority complex. Self deflation is the same as self inflation. One must come to terms with self! Jesus said one must deny self. ". . . if any man will come after me, let him deny himself, and take up his cross, and follow me" (Mt. 16:24). Yet one must affirm self before one can deny self. One cannot deny that which does not exist. "I don't think I can" comes from the deeper "I don't think I am". Why should anyone reject grace? There are many reasons. But the reason in this lesson — "I am not worthy of grace". "I am too unworthy to accept unearned, unmerited forgiveness." "Why should — how could anyone love me?" Only with good self esteem can admit needs, helplessness, and help! Self love will grasp grace!

Again, anyone who cannot give love cannot accept love! Love from such a one is worthless! If I am nothing then how could my love have value? Wherein is self love/esteem? Esteem comes from God. God created me — I am "one of a kind". God saved me in Christ at the cross. Price determines worth. The cross is God's value of me. *AMAZING GRACE!* This is why the cross (Gospel) is God's power to save (Rom. 1:15-17). Christianity is not philosophy. Facts do not, within themselves, give worth. One's esteem is in grace (1 Tim. 1:12-16). Christians are accepted in the beloved (Eph. 1:6). My being accepted changed me; I was not

61

changed to be accepted. In Christ I am free to be me. Eight times in 1, 2 Peter, Peter reminds us that God loves us! Love gives worth/esteem. One cannot reject what God has accepted.

I Believe In You

Trusting God, accepting self, allows one to believe in others. Trust is an imperative in life. One must trust God, himself, the significant others in life (family/friends), and the distant others in life (strangers). Christianity is not merely doctrinal facts; Christianity is relationship. Christianity is the ability to receive and give love. Christianity is the ability to make others better. Christians who doubt God and denigrate self cannot trust others. Insecured Christians cannot evangelize (Eph. 6:17). Assurance is the helmet of salvation. One, therefore, cannot evangelize "bare-headed". But to totally trust God and completely accept self frees one to believe in and serve others.

Take Barnabas, for instance. Satan's greatest tool is discouragement; man's greatest need is encouragement. Barnabas was the "Son of Encouragement". He renewed Saul and restored John Mark. He believed in others. Such a one is a magnet. Do you make people feel better? Do you leave a "good taste" in other's mouths?

Take Paul! Re-read our texts. Paul believed in himself, Onesimus, and Philemon. Trust is sacred! It frees one to become his best. Paul also believed in Corinth, Philippi, and Thessalonica. Paul always commended before he criticized. Paul brought out the best in others.

Take Jesus. He saw the "rock" in Peter, the integrity in Matthew. Jesus never put people down. Jesus gave the Great Commission to us (Mt. 28:18–20). He has no other plans! It is a sacred thought — Jesus trusts us.

We must trust. Preachers must trust preachers. There must be trust among elders, deacons, preachers, members. Parents must trust children! Children cannot be reared with constant criticism. They must know they are loved and trusted. Mates must know they are loved and trusted! Learn to have and live, "I believe in you".

A friend said humbly, "I just wish I could be the person you think I am". The answer, "I know, but the truth is you already are. My friendship does not require your perfection". When will we ever learn our worth is not in our knowledge and works? There is much more to one than function/production. Consider our aged/invalid. They feel they cannot be loved because they are shut-in. They must know they are loved and trusted without production! The greatest thing you can give is, "I love you and trust you completely". Love believeth all things (1 Cor. 13:7). Love trusts, hopes, and expects. "Wherefore receive ye one another, as Christ also received us to the glory of God. (Rom. 15:7). People will become what you expect them to. Leaders! Believe in yourselves! Lead! Believe in the congregation! They will fulfill any challenge that God wants done. *I BELIEVE IN YOU!*

Questions

1. Discuss in depth the reality and beauty of trust. Do we trust others? Do we make others look good?
2. Is it enough logically to prove "God is"? Is God good? Does God trust us? Want us? Prepare for us?
3. Is it scriptural to believe in one's self? Discuss pride, inverted pride. Discuss true self love. Wherein comes true self-esteem?
4. Discuss how we must trust each other. Give illustrations. Discuss relationship in Christianity.
5. Discuss Bible men who trusted/encouraged others.
6. Are you a "Cross-Bearer"?

Chapter Thirteen

Come, Lord Jesus

> "And I saw a new heaven and a new earth; for the first heaven and the first earth were passed away; and there was no more sea. And I, John, saw the holy city, new Jerusalem, coming down from God out of heaven, prepared as a bride adorned for her husband. And I heard a great voice out of heaven saying, Behold, the tabernacle of God is with men, and he will dwell with them, and they shall be his people, and God himself shall be with them, and be their God, and God shall wipe away all tears from their eyes: and there shall be no more death, neither shall there be any more pain: for the former things are passed away." (Revelation 21:1-4).

Can you remember the first night you spent away from your family? Things went well for a while, but then you began to get anxious about going back home. Perhaps a late night phone call awakened your parents. The message was clear . . . "I want to come home . . . O.K.?" That feeling in the pit of your stomach was what we call homesickness. Even adults can suffer this emotion: the daughter away at her first year in college: the son spending his first few days in the military, or the mate who is away from home on a trip. There's just something special about home. We would be upset if a family member didn't miss it!

Heaven!! . . . is God's word for home! Disciples of the Lord are homesick people. Our citizenship isn't on this planet. Our real home is in a special dwelling place God has especially prepared for his Children. Heaven will be our eternal home where the "gates swing outward never" and "where the soul of man never dies." We are here on an exciting mission for the King but our hearts are anxious for Homecoming Day! What a thrilling moment it will be when we hear the voice of our Lord beckon, ". . . come, ye blessed of my Father, inherit the Kingdom prepared for you from the foundation of the world." (Matthew 25:34)

Homesick Pilgrims
John

John, who pinned the final words of the Bible, was anxious to go home. He had served the Lord faithfully; he had caught a glimpse of what heaven was like in the visions of *Revelation*. His homesickness compelled him to shout, "Come, Lord Jesus!" (Revelation 22:20) Perhaps earlier words of Jesus flooded his mind:

> "Let not your hearts be troubled: ye; believe in God, believe also in me. In My Father's house are many mansions: if it were not so I would have told you. I go to prepare a place for you. And, if I go and prepare a place for you, I will come again, and receive you unto myself: that where I am, there ye may be also." (John 14:1-3)

John was missing his Father's house! He was ready to receive his reward.

Paul

Paul expressed this same attitude. He told Timothy that he was ready to die, but not because he was tired of his mission here on earth. He too, was homesick! (Philippians 3:20) He knew that "to live is Christ" but "to die is gain." (Philippians 1:21) His desire to go to heaven motivated him onward. (Philippians 3:13-20) It was his goal. In the closing words of I Corinthians we read very similar words as those spoken by John: "O Lord, Come!" (I Corinthians 16:22)

Heaven's Hall Of Fame Of Homesick Saints

The list of great servants of God in Hebrews 11 is often called "The Hall of Fame of Faith." Usually we teach lessons on "faith in God" from this Chapter and rightfully so, because these people were noted for their dynamic faith. But, their faith wasn't only in God. They also believe by faith that there was a special place awaiting them. These people admitted they were strangers, aliens here on earth; they were just sojourners.

> "These all died in their faith, not having received the promises, but having seen them afar off, and were persuaded of them, and embrased them, and confessed they were strangers and pilgrims on the earth. For they declared plainly that they seek a country. And truly if they had been mindful of that country from whence they came out, they might have had opportunity to have returned, But now they desire a better country, that is, a heavenly: wherefore God is not ashamed to be called their God: for he hath prepared for them a city." (Hebrews 11:13-16)

One of the faithful ones of Hebrews 11 was Abraham. The Bible states here that he sojourned in the land" (verse 9) and then verse 10 tells the reason why:

> "For he looked for a city which hath foundations, whose builder and maker is God."

Abraham was a homesick man! Perhaps this is one of the main reasons these people were so faithful. They wanted heaven more than anything in this world.

Twentieth Century Pilgrims

Baptized believers are the children of God by faith in Christ Jesus. And, in this new relationship are "Abraham's seed, and heirs according to the promise." (Galatians 3:26-29) We too are "strangers" (I Peter 1:1) and are to "pass the time of our sojourning here in fear" (I Peter 1:17) Like the disciples of the first century, we are to be "waiting" (I Thess. 1:10) and "watching" (I Thess. 5:6), and keeping ourselves busy preparing others for this same thing. (I Thess. 5:12-22; and II Thess. 3:6-16) As Christians we carry on the same mission and look for the same promises as the early disciples. We are to be busy doing the King's business, yet our hearts desired a city made by God!

But, what about we modern day disciples? Can we, do we pray, "Come, Lord Jesus."?? Someone has said, "we want to go to heaven . . . but, . . . not just yet!!" Our very spiritual strength can be measured by our attitude towards the second coming. Do we want Him to come? Next year? . . . Tomorrow? . . . Now??? If we do not wish this we are either unprepared to meet God, or we have grown to like our present "home" too much. Just how homesick are we?

Do We Really Want To Go Home?

The reason the believers we have read about were so anxious to go home was because they *saw, believed* and *embraced* the promises of such a place. (Hebrews 11:13) Even to them though there was the danger of losing sight of these things and failing to reach them. The Hebrew writer warned his listeners to hang on to these promises because Satan was always trying to deceive them into staying here!! (Hebrews 3:12-19) If we aren't homesick, then Satan has probably given us a good dose of his medicine. The label on the bottle has his usual prescription:

MATERIALISM — TAKE PLENTY OF TIME — DON'T EXPECT PERFECTION-TAKE LARGE DOSES DAILY . . . (Dr. Satan)

The apostle Peter has an extremely important message concerning this. He warns that in the last days Satan through his followers would attack God's promises to us:

"And saying, where is the promise of his coming: for since the fathers, all things continue as they were from the beginning of the creation." (II Peter 3:4)

Peter then challenges us not to be ignorant! God is still in control! Christ will come again! The Lord will come as a thief in the night! The heavens shall pass away. The elements and earth will be burned up! (II Peter 3:5-12) We must be cautious that Satan doesn't lead us astray. (Verse 17) Why? . . . Why is all of this so important to the disciple? Peter answers:

"Seeing then that all these *things* (includes materialism) shall be dissolved, what manner of persons ought ye to be in all holy living and godliness, *looking for and hasting unto the coming day of God* (there's homesickness) . . . nevertheless we, according to his *promise,* look for *new heavens and a new earth, wherein dwelleth righteousness.*" (there's our home)

(II Peter 3:11-13)

This passage focuses in on two of the poisonous ingredients in Satan's medicine. *"Things"* (our material possessions) will be completely destroyed and *"time"* is something we can't count on!!

The third ingredient in Satan's medicine is perhaps the most powerful, faith killer of all . . . "Don't expect perfection". In other words, "don't expect a resurrection."

The majority of mankind is sleeping under the ground! It is certain we too will die someday. (Hebrews 9:27) Satan wants to destroy our faith by having us believe we will always be in the grave! If we swallow this ingredient, we very well may begin "living like the Devil" for after all, we're told . . . "we only go around once." A Christian's belief in the resurrection of the dead is essential to their salvation! It is a powerful factor in this living the life of holiness Peter spoke of. If we don't really believe in the resurrection then we have destroyed our reason for shouting, "COME, LORD JESUS!!" This is the crux of the matter. Early believers based their faith on the empty tomb! The synoptic Gospels climax with this event; the epistles which were written during the time frame of *Acts* often refer to the prophets concerning the resurrection. Sermons throughout *Acts* focus on the Resurrection. (Acts 2; 3:15; 4:20; 5:30; 10:40; 13:30–37) *Revelation* is about victorious saints going to heaven. So the whole Bible is the Good news about our Savior who lived, served, bled and died for our sins on a cross, and on the third day arose victorious over death. In the act of baptism we took on the likeness of Christ and in that obedience told the world that we believed that as Christ was resurrected, we too will be resurrected at the second coming:

> "Know ye not, that so many of us as were baptized into Jesus Christ were baptized into his death? Therefore we are buried with him by baptism into death: that like as Christ was raised up from the dead by the glory of the Father, even so we also should walk in newness of life. For if we have been planted together in the likeness of his death, we shall be also in the likeness of his resurrection: " (Romans 6:3–5)

Yes, an obedient belief in the resurrection is essential for our salvation. We believe that just as Christ was raised out of his grave never to die again, we will experience this same victory. By God's power we shall "tear the bars away" and come forth to live a fresh life under new conditions of heavenly immortality. (Dan. 12:2; John 5:28–29)

Read all of I Corinthians 15. On resurrection morning every cemetery will be shaken! The prostrate dead will stand erect by Jesus' call. Our temples of clay will spring to life "in a moment, in the twinkling of an eye": physical corruption will yield to the transforming hand of God (verses 50–54); our dishonored, sickly houses of death will give away to celestial power, and we shall be changed, renewed and invigorated (verse 54); our new bodies will be galvanized against pain, sickness and death.

But why? why all this change? Because these are the bodies we go home in!!

"Beloved, now we are children of God, and it has not appeared as yet what we shall be. We know that if He should appear, We shall be like him, because we shall see Him just as He is" (I John 3:2)

From the judgment seat of God we will be sent into the heart of heaven. There we will see all the things *Revelation* describes and more. The tree of life will feed us; (Rev. 2:7) the terms sickness, death exist no more. The throne of God is there:

"And they shall see his face." (Rev. 22:3)

Conclusion

God wants us all to go home. He sent his son to die on the cross for this very purpose. In that supreme sacrifice he is "drawing" us unto himself. (John 12:32) It is our decision. The beauty of it all is that if only one person could be granted entrance to Heaven — we could be that one! Our belief and our hope is what motivates us to keep ourselves pure and holy in His sight:

"And every man that hath this hope in Him Purifieth himself, even as He is pure." (I John 3:3)

The deeper our faith and hope and love, the more homesick we become. As disciples of Christ we are anxious for the return of the Lord. We will rejoice when we hear the trumpet sound and see Him coming in the air. But, until that hour our spiritual condition must be such, that we regularly pray:

"COME, LORD JESUS."

Questions

1. Describe how you feel when someone prays, "Come Quickly Lord Jesus?"
2. We generally don't like the term "alien" . . . Why?
3. Someone has said, "we want to go to heaven . . . but, not just yet." Discuss.
4. The label on Dr. Satan's medicine usually reads" _____, _____, _____, take large doses _____. Discuss each of these.
5. Why is our belief in the resurrection so critical to our desiring the second coming?
6. Most graves face the East. What is the significance of this?
7. Is it possible to "hasten" the coming of the Lord?